The Great Prayer of
EPHESIANS

Frank Abissi Jr. Th.D., Ph.D.

WESTBOW
PRESS®
A DIVISION OF THOMAS NELSON
& ZONDERVAN

WestBow Press books may be ordered through booksellers or by contacting:

WestBow Press
A Division of Thomas Nelson & Zondervan
1663 Liberty Drive
Bloomington, IN 47403
www.westbowpress.com
1 (866) 928-1240

Interior Image Credit: Andrew S. Abissi

ISBN: 978-1-9736-8539-5 (sc)
ISBN: 978-1-9736-8538-8 (e)

Print information available on the last page.

WestBow Press rev. date: 3/31/2020

For Lena

Preface

Prayers and the answer to prayers have been a desire of God's people since man sinned and was banished from the Garden of Eden. The Bible has at least one prayer in 61 of its 66 books., for a total of nearly 1,100 prayers in the scriptures. The first record of prayers made by men is seen in Genesis.

> Genesis 4:26
> KJV
> [26] And to Seth, to him also there was born a son; and he called his name Enos: then began men to call upon the name of the LORD.

We do not know who specifically prayed or what these prayers were. The only thing we can be assured of is the fact that God heard their prayers. There is no record of how or if God answered their prayers. The scriptures do not tell us.

Man desires that his prayers be heard. Psalm 139 demonstrates the degree of intimacy of our relationship with God in prayer.

> Psalm 139
> KJV
> [1] O LORD, thou hast searched me, and known me.
> [2] Thou knowest my downsitting and mine uprising, thou understandest my thought afar off.
> [3] Thou compassest my path and my lying down, and art acquainted with all my ways.
> [4] For there is not a word in my tongue, but, lo, O LORD, thou knowest it altogether.
> [5] Thou hast beset me behind and before, and laid thine hand upon me.

[6] Such knowledge is too wonderful for me; it is high, I cannot attain unto it.

[7] Whither shall I go from thy spirit? or whither shall I flee from thy presence?

[8] If I ascend up into heaven, thou art there: if I make my bed in hell, behold, thou art there.

[9] If I take the wings of the morning, and dwell in the uttermost parts of the sea;

[10] Even there shall thy hand lead me, and thy right hand shall hold me.

[11] If I say, Surely the darkness shall cover me; even the night shall be light about me.

[12] Yea, the darkness hideth not from thee; but the night shineth as the day: the darkness and the light are both alike to thee.

[13] For thou hast possessed my reins: thou hast covered me in my mother's womb.

[14] I will praise thee; for I am fearfully and wonderfully made: marvellous are thy works; and that my soul knoweth right well.

[15] My substance was not hid from thee, when I was made in secret, and curiously wrought in the lowest parts of the earth.

[16] Thine eyes did see my substance, yet being unperfect; and in thy book all my members were written, which in continuance were fashioned, when as yet there was none of them.

[17] How precious also are thy thoughts unto me, O God! how great is the sum of them!

[18] If I should count them, they are more in number than the sand: when I awake, I am still with thee.

[19] Surely thou wilt slay the wicked, O God: depart from me therefore, ye bloody men.

[20] For they speak against thee wickedly, and thine enemies take thy name in vain.

[21] Do not I hate them, O LORD, that hate thee? and am not I grieved with those that rise up against thee?
[22] I hate them with perfect hatred: I count them mine enemies.
[23] Search me, O God, and know my heart: try me, and know my thoughts:
[24] And see if there be any wicked way in me and lead me in the way everlasting.

Jesus when asked, taught his disciples how to pray with the "Lord's Prayer". This particular prayer was never meant to be the end-all of prayers. It was the example Jesus used to teach his disciples.

Luke 11:1-4,9
KJV
[1] And it came to pass, that, as he was praying in a certain place, when he ceased, one of his disciples said unto him, Lord, teach us to pray, as John also taught his disciples.
[2] And he said unto them, When ye pray, say, Our Father which art in heaven, Hallowed be thy name. Thy kingdom come. Thy will be done, as in heaven, so in earth.
[3] Give us day by day our daily bread.
[4] And forgive us our sins; for we also forgive every one that is indebted to us. And lead us not into temptation; but deliver us from evil.
[9] And I say unto you, Ask, and it shall be given you; seek, and ye shall find; knock, and it shall be opened unto you.

To the Christian, prayers are intimate communications with our God. All great prayers fit into one of several categories as found in I Timothy.

I Timothy 2:1-4
KJV
[1] I exhort therefore, that, first of all, supplications, prayers, intercessions, and giving of thanks, be made for all men;
[2] For kings, and for all that are in authority; that we may lead a quiet and peaceable life in all godliness and honesty.
[3] For this is good and acceptable in the sight of God our Saviour;
[4] Who will have all men to be saved, and to come unto the knowledge of the truth.

Supplications are essentially requests for an object or service of necessity. Prayers show the longing in the heart of the one praying, be they for the necessity or of worship of our heavenly Father. Intercessions are prayers of necessity of another; for example, prayers of healing for another in a relationship with the one praying. The relationship can take on many different aspects, such as prayer for a leader in the body of Christ or a leader of another capacity. Prayer is not confined to an intimate relationship, but the one being prayed for need only to be known by the intercessor. Giving of thanks is self explanatory, except that the Holy Spirit qualified this prayer "be made for all men: For kings and for all that are in authority."(I Timothy 2:4)

The great prayer of the Epistle to the Ephesians is what binds the doctrinal treatises of the epistle with the practical treatises. It stands on its own in the midst of the epistle. The real power of this prayer begins with the bowing down before the majesty of God.

This book will bring the reader into the depths of this section of Ephesians (Ephesians 3:14-21). Philology presents an evidence-based research of the scriptures. This differs from a theological handling of the section by presenting the language studies, the figures of speech and studies of the Middle Eastern customs prevalent in the day.

The prayers that God desires of His family today are those that emanate from the heart, not the prayers that are produced through rote memory. His desire is for an honest and open communication from the seat of man's conscience i.e. the heart of a man. There is no prayer too petty or too great as we see at the end of the great prayer of Ephesians,

> Ephesians 3:20
> KJV
> [20] Now unto him that is able to do exceeding abundantly above all that we ask or think, according to the power that worketh in us,

Prayers of the Christian today are energized by the holy spirit within. And the sky is not anywhere close to being the limit.

Contents

Abstract

A Philological Examination Of The Great Prayer Of The Epistle To The Ephesians

The Great Prayer of Ephesians[1] is the pivotal point of the greatest revelation of God to the Church. Ephesians is the greatest revelation to the church as it reveals the Great Musterion, The Great Mystery, which is the foundation of the Church of God. As Ephesians has seven doctrinal and seven practical treatises, the Great Prayer is the fulcrum of the revelation.

The Prayer, when understood in respect to the greater context of the epistle, brings to light the connection between the doctrinal and practical. When the prayer is fully understood, the greatness of what God accomplished in Jesus Christ for the Church of the body is revealed.

This work examines the word constructions and figures of speech of the Great Prayer. Also, when applicable to the study, historical information and other evidence will be presented. This study presents an evidence-based study of the prayer.

---

[1] Ephesians 3:14ff

List of Charts

Statement of Consideration

As the Great Prayer of Ephesians is not considered part of either the Doctrinal or Practical Treatises, it has been treated as just an ancillary part of the Epistle. It has been viewed as being of less importance than other aspects of the Epistle. Most commentaries on Ephesians treat the prayer as a section to pass through as opposed to being valuable to dwell upon.

By looking at each verse individually and imparting a sense of importance to each, this work will bring to light the reason the Great Prayer is considered the pivotal section in Paul's epistle.

This work looks at a small portion of Ephesians (Ephesians 3:14-21), but it is perhaps the strongest section of God's Word as it pertains to the Church of the One Body. The section works as a pivotal section balancing both the doctrinal treatises (Ephesians 1:1-3:13) and the practical treatises (Ephesians 4:1-6:24). Whereas Romans was written primarily to the individual in Christ, Ephesians is written to the individual and his role in the great Church of the One Body. Understanding the Great Prayer in Ephesians will enable the Christian to link together the Great Musterion with his or her function in the body.

Thesis Statement

God placed the greatest importance on Paul's Epistle to the Ephesians. In this Epistle He reveals the Great Musterion, the framework of the Church of the Body of Christ. The Epistle itself is a cyclical epistle[2] and most probably is the lost epistle to the Laodiceans. Many believe that it is a Deutero-Pauline epistle, written by someone other than Paul, yet written in his voice. The Great Prayer of Ephesians acts as a bridge between the doctrinal and the practical treatises. It is the center of a perfectly balanced book meaning each doctrinal treatise coincides with a practical treatise.

Paul's intercessory prayer of Ephesians calls for understanding of the individual Christians, so they may be able to comprehend the fullness of the love of Christ which is beyond human understanding. There are two intercessory petitions in the prayer on behalf of the believers. The first petition is for establishment and the second is for the practical understanding of the Epistle. There are two prayers in Ephesians, the first in Ephesians 1:15-19a, and the second is the Great Prayer in Ephesians 3:14-21.

---

[2] Several of the epistles are cyclical in that they are never addressed to one particular church. The "to whom" the epistle is addressed is left blank by the writer. Romans and Galatians are two epistles not considered to be cyclical.

Definition of Terms

There are certain terms that are unique to Biblical studies that must be understood:

> Figure of Speech: A figure is utilized to bring color to an otherwise black and white book. A figure is a unique construction or description used in a section that calls importance to the section. Figures of speech can be thought of as the Holy Spirit's markings as to what is important. There are thought to be over nine hundred different figures of speech and as many as thirty different variations under them[3]
>
> Diligence must be utilized in the study of figures of speech, as not every apparent construction is always a figure of speech. Not every genitive construction will be a figure. A figure of speech will bring clarity, a sense of importance or attention to a section of scripture. An introversion construction can be considered a figure as it narrows down to the emphasis phrase or verse of a passage, however the alternation construction is not a figure.
>
> Deutero-Pauline: There is some dispute as to whether Paul wrote the epistle to the Ephesians. Some believe that someone else wrote the epistle, writing in a voice that is very similar to Paul's. It should be noted that the author of this dissertation believes that Paul originally wrote the epistle in Greek and very soon afterwards had it translated and written in Estrangelo Aramaic.

---

[3] See E.W. Bullinger; Figures of Speech used in the Bible for a basic idea of figures of speech. Over the years since Bullinger wrote this work more and different figures of speech have been found.

Biblical Philology is the study of ancient languages utilized in Biblical studies. It is a combination of history and linguistics, as well as translation and interpretation of Biblical texts and apocryphal writings as they relate to the received text of the Word of God. Philology also aspires to establish the authenticity of various texts. Biblical Philology takes into account historical records, archeological findings, manners and customs of ancient times in respect to the time and place and classes of the people to whom or from whom the written manuscript is related. Textual Criticism is a vital key to Philology. Certain texts carry more weight in respect to the translation as we search for an "original copy" of the text.

Word studies are utilized in that by looking at all the occurrences in the Bible first, and profane literature second, in order to find a proper definition and meaning of the word in relation to the context of which it appears. A word study brings to light the use and usages of a particular word and is of great use in the consideration of the word when presenting a translation. Sources of word studies used in this dissertation are Youngs Analytical Concordance of the Bible and The Word Study New Testament and Concordance.

Prayer: there are several different types of prayer found in the Bible.

I Timothy presents four different types:

I Timothy 2:1
KJV
[1] I exhort therefore, that, first of all, supplications, prayers, intercessions, and giving of thanks, be made for all men

Supplications are petitions to God for objects of need, quite literally they are requests for one's self. For example: "God help me" is a supplication. Another, προσευχὰς, is a request to God on behalf of another where the supplicant is prepared to relinquish all that he has in order to see that the person with need be filled by God. It is a type of prayer that brings in the notions of sacrifice, selfless generosity to help another. It is a very strong form of prayer. Intercessions are prayers to God on behalf of another. It is a very simple form of prayer similar to the innocent prayer of a child standing before God. The fourth form of prayer in this verse is the "giving of thanks" which stands self-explanatory.

Methods of Research

Research is considered to be an irritant to commonly established truth. For instance, every schoolchild learns that in the Middle Ages some considered the world to be flat. This study begins with the viewpoint that the Bible is the inspired and true Word of God. Any errors in understanding come from either a deficiency in our understanding or a problem with our translation. The author does not believe that there are any contradictions in the Bible, as God is perfect and therefore His Word must also be perfect. The basic premise of this work is that the Word of God is complete in itself, and there are no Biblical truths outside of it. The Bible is a complete package. A philological examination has at its root the concept that the Word of God will interpret itself, first, right where it is written. Interpretation can next be gleaned from the context. This cannot be ignored, as a redacting of the scriptures will result in the loss of the truth of the scriptures[4]. Each scripture must also be considered in light of where it has been used before. Each scripture must also be considered in light of figures of speech and also considered in light of what impact the customs of the day had upon what is written. The Bible is an Eastern book. Therefore it needs to be approached with an idea of the manners and customs of an Eastern civilization of the same time period.

Structures come from scope of the scriptures and not the other way around. Scope comes from reading the scriptures over and over. This sets the stage for the development of a structure of the text. Scope is particularly useful in the search for Figures of Speech used in the texts.

> II Peter 1:19ff
> KJV
> [19] We have also a more sure word of prophecy; whereunto ye do well that ye take heed, as unto a light

---

[4] Revelation 22:19

that shineth in a dark place, until the day dawn, and the day star arise in your hearts:

[20] Knowing this first, that no prophecy of the scripture is of any private interpretation.

[21] For the prophecy came not in old time by the will of man: but holy men of God spake as they were moved by the Holy Ghost.

Texts Utilized

At the beginning of each verse there are several different texts (translations) used. The reader needs to understand that translations fall on two different sides of the spectrum. Some promote what they believe to be the original thought of the Bible, while others are trying to present what they believe to be the original translation of the texts.

Textual Scale

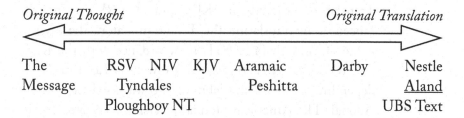

| Original Thought | | | | | Original Translation |

| The Message | RSV NIV KJV Tyndales Ploughboy NT | Aramaic Peshitta | Darby | Nestle Aland UBS Text |

The purpose of this scale is not to say that any known text is closest to being the actual text. Its purpose rather is to demonstrate the aim of the different versions and their particular importance to this study. Other texts are used in this study however they are not considered in relation to this scale. For example "The Phillips Modern Translation" is used but its frequency of usage is so small that it is not represented above.

The *William Tyndale Ploughboy Translation* was the first approved English Bible. Also known as the Matthew Bible, the Bible was approved for publication in 1537, several years after the death of William Tyndale. The purpose of the Bible was to make it very easy to read so that the ploughboys could read it at lunchtime.

The *King James Version* of 1611 is the most popular version of Scriptures that has ever been published. It attempts to adhere to the Stephens Text. Work on the version was begun in 1605 and completed in 1611. Because the Church of England developed the version it has a slight denominational slant to it. It is the first version to use a verse numerical identification system. Words added by the translators are in italics. The voice has an old English tone to it, causing many people to say that it is too difficult to read. It is used as the primary version in this study,

The *Revised Standard Version* is a revision of the American Standard Version. It was published throughout the twentieth century, with the final Protestant version being completed and first published in 1952. It utilized the 17th edition of the Nestle-Aland Text. There were three major points that the RSV was designed to cover.

1. Translators utilized the KJV and the RV's standard procedure of translating the Tetragrammaton, the divine name of Yahweh (YHWH) in accordance with the KJV and RV'. The RSV translated Yahweh as Lord or God depending upon which Hebrew word was used Elohim or Adonai. The American Standard Version translated these words as Jehovah.

2. Probably the most important change for the English reader was the change of translation of the second-person pronouns such as "thou, thy, thee, hast etc." The RSV reserves the use of the archaic pronouns and verbs solely for addressing God. This seemed to become a universal practice among translators until 1977.

3. The RSV utilized the latest version of the Nestle-Aland text, whereas the KJV used the Textus Receptus (The Stephens Text). The RV and the ASV had utilized the Wescott and Hort Greek New Testament.

Darby Bible was originally titled "The Holy Scriptures: a New Translation from the Original Languages" by J.N. Darby, published originally in 1867 the Bible was revised in 1872 and 1884. Darby only translated the New Testament. After his death, several of his students took upon themselves the task of producing an Old Testament based on Darby's French and German translations. Darby's purpose in producing the New Testament he mentions in his preface was to make a modern translation for the unlearned that, have neither access to MSS nor the training and knowledge of ancient languages of the scriptures. Darby was the principal scholar for a number of translations in his day.

The Peshitta Aramaic Translation, as completed by Janet Magiera, follows closely to the Estrangelo and the Syriac MSS. This translation became available in 2003. This translation is used, as it remains closer to the Aramaic manuscripts available. The George Lamsa Aramaic Bible was considered as a source, however it lacks features such as italics, and does not follow the text fully. (For example in Romans 15, the order of verses is different in the Aramaic than in the Greek. The Peshitta follows the order of the verses, while Lamsa tries to recover the figure of speech present in the Greek).

Over one hundred scholars utilizing the "best" manuscripts available wrote the New International Version[5]. The writers used Greek, Aramaic, and Hebrew Manuscripts in the translation. This version of the scriptures was the development of fifteen scholars who took upon themselves the task of compilation of the text. A General Electric engineer by the name of Howard Long started the project. He had been a lifelong devotee of the King James Version but found that when he presented the scriptures to his friends they had a very difficult time connecting with the King James English.

The Nestle-Aland text has been the standard Greek text for many years and is still considered one of the two standardized Greek texts used by theologians (The other is the United Bible Societies text). The text is currently in its 28th edition with the 29th edition currently in the works. The 28th was published in the 114th year since the publishing of the 1st edition.

---

[5] There are several different methods of textual criticism utilized by various scholars. With over 100 people working on the texts, it is hard to determine which MSS to which they gave the most weight.

The United Bible Societies Greek text Third Edition (1975) is unique in its text being somewhat similar to the Stephens text from which the Authorized King James Version of 1611 was produced. Over forty Greek Scholars, including Bruce Metzger, who was in charge of the work, researched the apparatus. The apparatus and the companion textual work by Bruce Metzger[6] make this text and apparatus the most comprehensive on the market at the time of this writing.

Each version utilized in this study brings with it a unique perspective of the text. It is with this usage of various texts that an Expanded Translation can be rendered.

---

[6] Metzger, Bruce M. A Textual Commentary On The Greek New Testament. London-New York, United Bible Societies 1971

Review of Literature

There is one other book available in English today that specifically deals with the prayers of Ephesians and that is "The Prayers of Ephesians" by E.W. Bullinger. This book is a very straightforward view of the two prayers and were most likely sermons written by Bullinger.

Many guides to study that contain sections on the prayers of Ephesians have been written over the years, however none seem to present very valid information for the serious student of the epistle. Each of these has at its root the idea that the interpretation of the scriptures is latent within the man. Most of these are not based upon legitimate methods of research. Many believe that there are many different interpretations of any section of scriptures, however one wishes to interpret it is correct. If this is true then there is no need for researching of the scriptures and really no reason for the scriptures at all. This is a foundational idea of Pantheism.[7]

---

[7] Pantheism is the belief that the Universe and all that is contains within nature is identical with the divine. It also believes that totality of nature makes up the divine and the all encompassing, natural world is god. Pantheists do not believe in a distinct and personal god or anamorphic god. It is the full and complete research of nature.

Recommendations for Future Research

There are several prayers in the church epistles. Each is unique in character and unique in the petitions they request. A complete chart outlining each prayer and the relationship they present to other prayers in the Grace Administration would be useful. Also valuable would be a comparative compilation of the prayers in Ephesians, Philippians, and Colossians, as these three epistles are related as doctrine, reproof and corrections and fall under the category of the individual in relationship to the church of God. This shows their individual function in the body of Christ.

Prefatory Notes

1. The Greek font used in this dissertation is called SPIonic [SPIonic]. The font can be downloaded to one's computer at **http://rosetta.reltech.org/TC/fonts**
2. Textual variants are discussed where applicable[8].
3. LXX is the abbreviation of the Septuagint. It is called such, as 70 men were the translator/writers of the text.

---

[8] Metzger, Bruce M. A Textual Commentary On The Greek New Testament. London-New York, United Bible Societies 1971 is the major work from which the variants are found and cited

Ephesus in 55-70 A.D.

II Timothy 1:16-18
KJV
[**16**] The Lord give mercy unto the house of Onesiphorus; for he oft refreshed me, and was not ashamed of my chain:[**17**] But, when he was in Rome, he sought me out very diligently, and found me.
[**18**] The Lord grant unto him that he may find mercy of the Lord in that day: and in how many things he ministered unto me at Ephesus, thou knowest very well.

II Timothy 4:9-12
KJV
[**9**] Do thy diligence to come shortly unto me:
[**10**] For Demas hath forsaken me, having loved this present world, and is departed unto Thessalonica; Crescens to Galatia, Titus unto Dalmatia.
[**11**] Only Luke is with me. Take Mark, and bring him with thee: for he is profitable to me for the ministry.
[**12**] And Tychicus have I sent to Ephesus.

The Epistle to the Ephesians is traditionally considered to have been written in A.D. 62 AD. However, critical scholars have questioned the authorship of the letter to a Deutero-Pauline authorship with a writing in A.D.80.

The Apostle John was said to have spent much of his life in Ephesus. This fact however is under dispute, as there are very few scriptural or historical documents to support this.

The Great Prayer of Ephesians

Ephesians 3:14-21
King James Version
[14] For this cause I bow my knees unto the Father of our Lord Jesus Christ,

[15] Of whom the whole family in heaven and earth is named,

[16] That he would grant you, according to the riches of his glory, to be strengthened with might by his Spirit in the inner man;

[17] That Christ may dwell in your hearts by faith; that ye, being rooted and grounded in love,

[18] May be able to comprehend with all saints what is the breadth, and length, and depth, and height;

[19] And to know the love of Christ, which passeth knowledge, that ye might be filled with all the fulness of God.

[20] Now unto him that is able to do exceeding abundantly above all that we ask or think, according to the power that worketh in us,

[21] Unto him be glory in the church by Christ Jesus throughout all ages, world without end. Amen.

This prayer is the second prayer of Paul in this letter to the Ephesians[9]. This prayer is an intercessory prayer from Paul to God. Often intercessory prayer is regarded as a defense for sin. In this case it is for the building

---

[9] This Epistle is regarded as a cyclical letter, it was never to be regarded as a letter solely to the ones at Ephesus. See "The Doctrine of Ephesians" for a further explanation.

FRANK ABISSI JR. TH.D., PH.D.

up of the saints and would have to be considered a necessary and vital function of Paul's ministry as an Apostle of Jesus Christ.

> Ephesians 4:11,12
> KJV
> [11] And he gave some, apostles; and some, prophets; and some, evangelists; and some, pastors and teachers;
> [12] For the perfecting of the saints, for the work of the ministry, for the edifying of the body of Christ:

Paul's purpose in this prayer is a request to God that He would impart to the believers His power, and to put into their hearts an awareness of the internal reality of His true presence. Paul desires an outpouring of God's Love and His divine power into the hearts of the saints. The solemn introduction that Paul makes for the prayer gives the great weight to the prayer that is so rightfully deserves.

The opening words of this prayer show that Paul had some great concerns regarding the Gentiles. Paul begins the section that is the revelation of the Great Musterion with the words "for this cause". He quickly changes the subject though and begins discussing his purpose in the stewardship the of the Great Musterion, and the distinct place the Gentiles had in their sharing of the Musterion as God had revealed it to Paul.

Before the day of Pentecost, sin was man's greatest problem. Jesus Christ was the payment for sin. He was the Passover Lamb. Today the problem is not sin but rather the sinner. The Great Prayer of Ephesians does not address the sin problem of the world. It is taking on the concept that man was made righteous by Jesus Christ, and in Ephesians is a moving away from the idea of sin[10]. Ephesians deals with the individual and his place within the family and church of God. Romans spends most of the time dealing with the individual in a state of sin. E.W. Bullinger states that the writing of Romans is the "Grace" while the writing

---

[10] See I John 2:1

of Ephesians is the Fruit[11]. The first petition in the first prayer of Ephesians is concerning God's inheritance:

> Ephesians 1:11
> KJV
> [11] In whom also we have obtained an inheritance, being predestinated according to the purpose of him who worketh all things after the counsel of his own will:

All the blessings of God are sealed in the individual by the Holy Spirit when we believed, not "after" we believed as the KJV. There is no "after" present in the Greek. The Nestle- Aland Text (Edition 2) literally reads "in whom, ye also, on believing, were sealed". Both are Aorist participles, properly translated as *on hearing* and *on believing* and *when ye believed*.

> Ephesians 1:13
> KJV
> [13] In whom ye also trusted, after that ye heard the word of truth, the gospel of your salvation: in whom also after that ye believed, ye were sealed with that holy spirit of promise.

There are some major differences between this prayer and the Great Prayer of Ephesian. For example the first prayer is addressed to God, while this second prayer is addressed to the Father. The first prayer petitions God for enlightenment of the inner man, while the second petitions Him for the strengthening of the inner man. Both prayers ask God for knowledge only the first is asking for the knowledge of God and the hope of His calling, the second petitions God for the knowledge of Christ. In the first prayer, we are in Christ while in the second it is Christ in us. Though there are a few parallels in both prayers, they are still both very different in scope and purpose. The duplicity of the

---

[11] Bullinger, E.W.; The Prayers of Ephesians: Decatur, MI Invictus. No Copyright.

prayers is not to be considered as a confirmation of one another as each is able to stand on its own.

There are four distinct elements of this prayer: 1. Address and Glorification, 2. First intercessory petition. 3 Second intercessory petition 4. Doxology.[12]

---

[12] Some authors believe that there are three intercessory petitions in this prayer (i.e., Charles H. Welch). The reasoning is the fact that the word ἵνα is used three times in the prayer and this word sets the start of each petition

Ephesians 3:14-21 Introversion and Alternation

A. Address and Glorification Eph. 3:14,15
　B. Intercession #1 on behalf of the saints - Establishment Eph 3:16,17
　　a. To be granted according to the riches of His grace Eph 3:16
　　　a. To be strengthened with might
　　　　b. by His spirit
　　　a. In the inner man
　　b. For Christ to dwell in your heart by believing Eph 3:17
　B. Intercession #2 on behalf of the saints – Practical Eph 3:18,19
　　a. To comprehend with all saints Eph 3:18
　　　a. Understanding God's great power
　　　　b. Understanding depth of the love of Christ
　　　a. Filled with all fulness of God
　　b. To experientially know the love of Christ Eph 3:19
A. Doxology Eph 3:20,21

The first Intercessory petition contains three different independent elements.

1. To be strengthened with might
2. By His spirit
3. In the inner man (In the heart of the man)

The second Intercessory petition calls for an understanding of two elements

1. Understanding of God's great power
2. Understanding of the depth of the love of Christ
3. Filled with all the fulness of God (Capsulation of #1&2)

There are three reasonings that Paul makes for these intercessory petitions. Each begins with the Greek word for "that" – ἵνα. they are as follows:

Three Reasoning for intercessory prayer

1. That He would grant you
2. That Christ may dwell in your hearts by believing
3. That you being rooted and grounded in Love

looking at Ephesians as three separate and distinct section, Doctrinal, The Great Prayer, and the Practical section. After the instruction of the seven doctrinal treatises one enters the inner sanctum as presented in The Great Prayer. Paul's desire is that all the saints, the faithful ones in Christ Jesus, have an unprecedented relationship with the Father. An understanding of the doctrine is required, and the Great Prayer of Eph. 3:14-21 requests of God that the believer understand doctrine (with the help of God). It is only through this relationship that the believer can gain an understanding of the seven doctrinal treatises. While this prayer could, for all intents, stand alone, the purpose of it in Ephesians is to bridge the doctrinal treatises with the practical treatises. As such, the prayer presents aspects of both.

Deutero-Pauline Argument

There are seven epistles that are considered to be of true Pauline authorship. They are: Romans, I & II Corinthians, Galatians, Philippians, I Thessalonians, and Philemon. The epistle to the Hebrews is of anonymous authorship, as is generally accepted in theological circles. Six additional letters, which contain Paul's name as the author, do not currently enjoy the same academic consensus: Ephesians, Colossians, II Thessalonians, I & II Timothy, and Titus. The first three, called the "Deutero-Pauline Epistles," have no consensus on whether or not they are authentic letters of Paul. These epistles are part of the group of epistles considered to be church epistles. The second three make up the Pastoral Epistles. The anonymity of the author of Hebrews gives contemporary scholars reason to reject a Pauline authorship. The voice of the epistle is considerably different than that of the church epistles putting John as a possibility of being the author. Concerning the Deutero-Pauline epistles, it is possible that a later authorship occurred and during those years Paul's voice in his writings changed. This makes for a very good argument for a Pauline authorship. Though the pinpointing of the authorship is necessary to the validity of the epistle, truly the author of these epistles is God while Paul is the writer.

> II Timothy 3:16.17
> RSV
> [16] All scripture is inspired by God and profitable for teaching, for reproof, for correction, and for training in righteousness,
> [17] that the man of God may be complete, equipped for every good work.

Galatians 1:8-13

RSV

[8] But even if we, or an angel from heaven, should preach to you a gospel contrary to that which we preached to you, let him be accursed.

[9] As we have said before, so now I say again, If anyone is preaching to you a gospel contrary to that which you received, let him be accursed.

[10]Am I now seeking the favor of men, or of God? Or am I trying to please men? If I were still pleasing men, I should not be a servant of Christ.

11]For I would have you know, brethren, that the gospel which was preached by me is not man's gospel.

[12] For I did not receive it from man, nor was I taught it, but it came through a revelation of Jesus Christ.

Comparing the voice and grammatical idiosyncrasies, such as Paul's propensity for very long, run out sentences (The Great Prayer is only one sentence) with the authorized Pauline Epistles, one can conclude that Paul is the writer of Ephesians. Paul also uses a combination of Alternation and Introversion structures frequently in the Epistles, which seems to be a signature of his. Some of the confusion could lie in the fact that Paul had the Epistles translated into Aramaic very shortly after they were written in Greek. The figures of speech and many of the grammatical constructs that Paul wrote into the Greek are either nonexistent or very different in the Syriac. Paul's background as a former member of the Sanhedrin[13] would have made Hebrew Paul's first language though he was also a very proficient and fluent speaker of Greek.

Paul also had Roman citizenship. With his credentials, he seemed to have no problem using them for his furtherance of the Gospel. If Paul did not translate the epistles into Aramaic himself this difference between the Greek and the Aramaic would definitely bring about the reason for the idea of a different writer of Ephesians.

---

[13] See Acts 8, There are several more sections of scriptures that discuss Paul's pedigree. In these verses he is exercising his authority as a full member of the Sanhedrin.

Ephesians 3:14
King James Version
[14] For this cause I bow my knees unto the Father of our Lord Jesus Christ,

Ephesians 3:14
Revised Standard Version
[14] For this reason I bow my knees before the Father,

Ephesians 3:14
New International Version
[14] For this reason I kneel before the Father,

Ephesians 3:14
Aramaic Peshitta Version
[14] and I bow my knees to the Father of our Lord Yeshue-Meshikha,

Ephesians 3:14
Darby Translation (1890)
[14] For this reason I bow my knees to the Father *of our Lord Jesus Christ.*

This verse begins the pivotal section of Ephesians, the Great Prayer that sets itself as the focus of the epistle and the separation of the doctrinal and practical treatises. Recalling that Ephesians is a perfectly balanced book, presenting seven doctrinal and seven practical treatises, the Great Prayer is the fulcrum point between them.[14]

---

[14] Abissi, Frank.: The Doctrine of Ephesians, Parker, CO. Outskirts Publishing. 2015 pg. 26. Also see Appendix One

This verse begins with "For this cause" which refers back to the subject of Ephesians 3:1. This sets it as the figure of speech "Anachoresis"[15] or a regression to the original subject after a digression. The subject of Ephesians 3:1-13 is The Great Mystery. This is the digression to which this figure of speech refers.

> Ephesians 3:1
> KJV
> [1] For this cause I Paul, the prisoner of Jesus Christ for you Gentiles,

Leaving out the Parembole (further information) of v2-13, the text could read as such and bringing the two together the text could read as follows:

> Ephesians 3:1,14
> KJV
> [1] For this cause I Paul, a prisoner of Jesus Christ for you all
> [14] For this cause I Paul bow my knees unto the Father of our Lord Jesus Christ

The cause that is discussed here goes back to the final verses of chapter 2, the building together for a habitation of God, The Holy Temple in the Lord.

> Ephesians 2:20ff
> KJV
> [20] And are built upon the foundation of the apostles and prophets, Jesus Christ himself being the chief corner stone;
> [21] In whom all the building fitly framed together groweth unto an holy temple in the Lord:

---

[15] Bullinger, E.W.: The Companion Bible. Grand Rapids, MI. Zondervan Bible Publishers. 1974 Appendix 6 – pg. 8

[22] In whom ye also are builded together for an habitation of God through the Spirit.

Each version of this verse has slight but significant differences and presents the argument of whether this is prayer is to God, the Father of our Lord Jesus Christ, or is it addressed to God as the Father of us all. The King James Version (KJV) and the Aramaic Peshitta Version address the prayer to God, the Father of our Lord Jesus Christ while the Revised Standard Version (RSV) and the New International Version (NIV) address the prayer to God, The Father -The Father of all that are a part of the family of God. The Darby Translation (DARBY) sets the words "of our Lord Jesus Christ" in italics. Here Darby is distinguishing these words as added by translators and not appearing in the MSS's from which he derived his translation.

Given that the previous doctrinal sections of Ephesians deal with the Great Mystery, this verse would not distinguish out the Family of God and suddenly forget that we are joint heirs with Christ and part of the body of Christ.

> Ephesians 3:6
> KJV
> [6] That the Gentiles should be fellowheirs, and of the same body, and partakers of his promise in Christ by the gospel:

This section of scripture begins immediately after a Parembole consisting of Verses 2-13[16]. Another figure of speech starts off the prayer section. It is an Ellipsis, relative of the cognate words. The verb 'prayer' is supplied from the noun. Without the Ellipsis it would read: "Praying that he would grant you". This is the literal translation of "bowing my knees." The verbal "praying" is alluded to by the action of bowing the knees. There is basically no other reason for the bowing of the knees other than prayer and worship.

---

[16] A Parembole is a figure of speech that is further information by way of insertion.

FRANK ABISSI JR. TH.D., PH.D.

There is another figure of speech here in the verse. Anachoresis is a return to the original subject after a digression. The presence of this figure is verified by the fact that Verses 2-13 is a Parembole. The Latins called this verse a Regressio (or regression). The Greeks called it "Epanaclesis" which broken down means ἐπί – 'upon' ἀνά which translates to 'back' and κλησιζ 'a calling'. Hence the figure is a "calling back upon", or "a recalling".

Because this prayer is the focal point of the epistle to the Ephesians, one would expect a greater number of figures of speech than in other portions of the text. The figure of speech is the Holy Spirit's markings of what should draw ones attention, to show what carries more weight and is of great importance.

Jewish prayers were primarily offered standing up. Occasionally they were offered kneeling or prostrate in the Old Testament. As their custom, Gentiles usually prostrated themselves only before emperors and rulers. Greeks rarely if ever knelt to pray. Archeological findings at Laodicea and Ephesus show certain cultic religions, which were known to exist, had the adherents on their knees though the ceremony. Similar to the manner in which the Jews stretched out their arms with their palms facing up toward the heavens, the Gentiles (pagan worshippers) are seen as facing the gods they were invoking as their manner of prayer[17]

> I Kings 8:54
> KJV
> [54] And it was so, that when Solomon had made an
> end of praying all this prayer and supplication unto the
> LORD, he arose from before the altar of the LORD,
> from kneeling on his knees with his hands spread up
> to heaven.

---

[17] Quite often their prayers were directed toward statues, or the seas (gods of the waters i.e., Neptune).

The usual posture for prayer among Jews and Gentiles was standing. When bowing, it brought a weight to the prayer that was beyond the usual daily prayers.

In the Eastern world there were six different positions of bowing. The type of bow depended upon to whom the bow was directed and the relationship between the one bowing and the recipient of the bow. For example a servant in an everyday relationship with a master would use positions #1 and #2. Pose #3 and #4 demonstrate humility to one greater. Paul here is talking about a position of great thankfulness and humility to God so position #5 would be the bow specifically used in this application.

Position #6 is used as a bow of complete humility. It cannot be the bow used here. The social conventions of the day point to #5 as being the bowing of the knees. The Eastern man would never put his face so close to the ground as culturally it is not something that is done.

In Matthew 23 we hear Jesus reprove the Pharisees in their manner of prayer. The idea was that widows were unable to take care of their own affairs without a husband. The Pharisees would pray in the temple for the widow. The idea was that the one who made the longest prayer for the widow was the one who was believed to be the one chosen by the Lord to take care of her affairs. What a Pharisee did after the long prayer spoke to their nature of taking advantage of the widow. Once they had control of her estate, he would then rob it in the name of helping the widow.

Matthew 23:14
KJV
[14] Woe unto you, scribes and Pharisees, hypocrites! for
ye devour widows' houses, and for a pretence make long
prayer: therefore ye shall receive the greater damnation.

This is the reason why God spoke about the need for the care of widows
in I Timothy 5.

I Timothy 5:3-5
KJV
[3] Honour widows that are widows indeed.
[4] But if any widow have children or nephews, let them
learn first to shew piety at home, and to requite their
parents: for that is good and acceptable before God.
[5] Now she that is a widow indeed, and desolate,
trusteth in God, and continueth in supplications and
prayers night and day.

It is of note that God answers prayer, however a conscience is a necessary
element. Prayer demonstrates man's inability and God's ability to supply
the items of necessity. As pointed out earlier there are four types of
prayers: intercessions, supplications prayers and giving of thanks.
Colossians demonstrates the effects of prayer:

Colossians 1:9-11
KJV
[9] For this cause we also, since the day we heard it, do
not cease to pray for you, and to desire that ye might be
filled with the knowledge of his will in all wisdom and
spiritual understanding;
[10] That ye might walk worthy of the Lord unto
all pleasing, being fruitful in every good work, and
increasing in the knowledge of God;

[11] Strengthened with all might, according to his glorious power, unto all patience and longsuffering with joyfulness;

Here we find that Paul's prayer for the Colossians was the desire that they become as verses 10 and 11 state. Paul's understanding once again is that the limitless ability and resources of God could bring these things to pass.

The words "God the Father" are used to distinguish God as The Father in a most honored position as the supreme Father of all. Πατέρ is indicative of the relationship which connotes "son"[18] as the object of the relationship. This word also denotes a parent-child relationship. It is not indicative of "offspring" therefore it can be used of adopted children. It is also sometimes used as a wider meaning of senior, ancestor, pillar or founder.

This prayer, like its counterpart, sees many words for "power". God's mighty activity is stressed, first by means of the relatively rare Greek word rendered "strengthen" (κραταιόω means to become strong, to become powerful. The passive voice here draws attention to God's activities and expression of His power. This verb is used only four times in the New Testament and is not found in the LXX[19]). The phrase "with power" was a Hebrew expression[20].

Psalm 65:6
[6] Which by his strength setteth fast the mountains; being girded **with power**

---

[18] Daughters are inclusive here in that relationship.

[19] Hatch, Edwin and Redpath, Henry A., A Concordance of the Septuagint and other Greek versions of the Old Testament including the Apocryphal Books. In Two Volumes.; Grand Rapids, MI Baker Book House Vol 2

[20] O'Brien, Peter T.; The Letter To The Ephesians. Grand Rapids, MI. Wm B. Eerdmans Publishing Co. pg. 257

Luke 4:32
[32] And they were astonished at his doctrine: for his word was **with power**.

Romans 1:4
[4] And declared to be the Son of God **with power**, according to the spirit of holiness, by the resurrection from the dead:

Each of these verses could be considered Figures of Speech as the words "with power" should be considered redundant.

The words *"of our Lord Jesus Christ"* are absent from the Nestle Aland and the United Bible Societies texts

Ephesians 3:14
Expanded Translation
[14] For this reason (as I spoke afore) I bow my knees in thankfulness and humility to God, The Father.

Ephesians 3:15
KJV
[15] Of whom the whole family in heaven and earth is named,

Ephesians 3:15
RSV
[15] from whom every family in heaven and on earth is named,

Ephesians 3:15
NIV
[15] from whom every family in heaven and on earth derives its name.
Ephesians 3:15

Ephesians 3:15
Aramaic Peshitta Version
[15] from whom all the family which is in heaven and on earth is named,

Ephesians 3:15
DARBY
[15] of whom every family in *the* heavens and on earth is named.

Ephesians 3:15
Tyndales Plowboy Translation
[15] of whom each fatherhood in heavens and in earth
is named, [of whom each fatherhood in heaven and in
earth is named,]

This verse deals with a quality surname. It deals with just one family
group, the family of God. The RSV, NIV, and DARBY translate it
by trying to bring about the idea of different families in Heaven. The
Greek πασα should be translated "as all, without separation". It has
a connotation of unity – one. On earth there may be a separation of
families, but in heaven it is one family, with God as THE FATHER.
The reality of the one family is established by the Great Musterion as
revealed in Ephesians 3:6.

It is important that the previous prayer in Ephesians be compared, and
a careful consideration of similarities must be observed. In both prayers
there are references to 'a name'. This sets a distinction to whom the
prayers are addressed

Ephesians 1:21
KJV
[21] Far above all principality, and power, and might,
and dominion, and every name that is named, not only
in this world, but also in that which is to come:

Ephesians 3:15
KJV
[15] Of whom the whole family in heaven and earth is
named,

In the Book of Acts, Paul references an unknown God that the
Athenians were worshipping.

Acts 17:22,23

KJV

[22] Then Paul stood in the midst of Mars' hill, and said, Ye men of Athens, I perceive that in all things ye are too superstitious.

[23] For as I passed by, and beheld your devotions, I found an altar with this inscription, TO THE UNKNOWN GOD. Whom therefore ye ignorantly worship, him declare I unto you.

The Ancient world was very religious and very pagan in its thought. It was truly a polytarian (many gods) society.

Both realms, the physical (earth) and the spiritual (heavens) are brought up in verse 15. In the physical realm every man has an earthly father, but in the spiritual realm we all have the same Father – God.

The word family, πατρία is a play on the previous Father, πατήρ, and gives the idea for any group to be derived from a single ancestor. In the LXX it is used for family (Lamech, Tubal-Cain etc.), tribe (i.e. Dan) or even nation (Israel, Philistines, Jesuits). Its usage here in Ephesians indicates it is in reference to every family grouping into one Family of God. It is important to be aware of the fact that the Greek and the English ideas of family are slightly different. The English word for family is derived from the Latin *Famulus* or "the servant" while the Greek uses πατρία which has its root in the word πατέρ translated into English as "Father". In a practical sense this means that the Latin family goes beyond the blood relation confines to include certain servants within the family group, while the Greek concept of family was members within the blood relationship (and adoption) confines. The Greeks went so far as to require an oath to unite the family group together religiously. This oath had the sons and daughters of the family obey the father of the family without qualification[21]. God requires an oath of the Believers who join His family.

---

[21] Kittel, Gerhard: Theological Dictionary Of The New Testament. Grand Rapids, MI. Wm. B. Eerdmans Publishing Company. 1964, Vol 5, pg. 949

FRANK ABISSI JR. TH.D., PH.D.

Romans 10:8-11
RSV
[8] But what does it say? The word is near you, on your lips and in your heart (that is, the word of faith which we preach);
[9] because, if you confess with your lips that Jesus is Lord and believe in your heart that God raised him from the dead, you will be saved.
[10] For man believes with his heart and so is justified, and he confesses with his lips and so is saved.
[11] The scripture says, "No one who believes in him will be put to shame."

The Greek patriarchal model of the family believes that Zeus was the father of the gods. All the gods of Olympus were required to pledge their allegiance to him. It is also very important to note that this is the only occurrence of the word πατρια being translated as "Family" in the New Testament". As a matter of fact, it is used only three times in New Testament

Luke 2:4
KJV
[4] And Joseph also went up from Galilee, out of the city of Nazareth, into Judaea, unto the city of David, which is called Bethlehem; (because he was of the house and lineage (patria) of David:)

Luke 2:25
KJV
[25] Ye are the children of the prophets, and of the covenant which God made with our fathers, saying unto Abraham, And in thy seed shall all the kindreds (patria) of the earth be blessed.

Both of these verses support the Greek idea of family being of a seed relationship. The lineage of David was closely watched as the Savior was supposed to be a descendent from the house of David. God's promise to Abraham was that his seed would be as the stars of heaven.

> Genesis 25:3-5
> KJV
> [3] Sojourn in this land, and I will be with thee, and will bless thee; for unto thee, and unto thy seed, I will give all these countries, and I will perform the oath which I sware unto Abraham thy father;
> [4] And I will make thy seed to multiply as the stars of heaven, and will give unto thy seed all these countries; and in thy seed shall all the nations of the earth be blessed;
> [5] Because that Abraham obeyed my voice, and kept my charge, my commandments, my statutes, and my laws.

In an Eastern family home, the inside is divided into separate areas for each particular family unit. Each son when he was married would have one of these partitioned sections of the home where he and his wife, family would live. Each was similar to an apartment.

> John 14:2
> KJV
> [2] In my Father's house are many mansions [apartments, living spaces]: if it were not so, I would have told you. I go to prepare a place for you.

It is of particular importance to note the reckoning of family names. Sons are known by the name of their father. For instance, "Jesus Bar-Joseph" is Jesus the son of Joseph. Jesus Barabbas, the robber that was pardoned instead of Jesus Christ, was "the son of the father".[22] All the

---

[22] Judges 5 discusses Barak. It has been taught in some circles that this is alluding to "a son of Ak" however Judges 4:6 clears this up by naming him Barak Bar-Abinoam. Consider also Jeremiah 32:12 Baruch Bar-Neriah. Matthew10:3 James Bar-Alphaeus. Shows that the custom of the name of the father taken carries throughout the scriptures.

FRANK ABISSI JR. TH.D., PH.D.

sons that lived in the house of their father (John 14:2) would have the name surname Bar- (Insert fathers name). Even today the Sherpa from Nepal take their fathers name as their surname while their given name is the name of the day of the week in which they were born[23].

Besides the name of their father, a family group was known by the ancestors or lineage from which they came. For example, the Gospel of Matthew begins with stating the familiar line or lineage of Jesus

> Matthew 1:1
> KJV
> [1] The book of the generation of Jesus Christ, the son of David, the son of Abraham.

The book then goes on to name the lineage as being pure from Abraham, to David to Jesus.

> Matthew 1:2-17
> KJV
> 2] Abraham begat Isaac; and Isaac begat Jacob; and Jacob begat Judas and his brethren;
> [3] And Judas begat Phares and Zara of Thamar; and Phares begat Esrom; and Esrom begat Aram;
> [4] And Aram begat Aminadab; and Aminadab begat Naasson; and Naasson begat Salmon;
> [5] And Salmon begat Booz of Rachab; and Booz begat Obed of Ruth; and Obed begat Jesse;
> [6] And Jesse begat David the king; and David the king begat Solomon of her that had been the wife of Urias;
> [7] And Solomon begat Roboam; and Roboam begat Abia; and Abia begat Asa;
> [8] And Asa begat Josaphat; and Josaphat begat Joram; and Joram begat Ozias;

---

[23] Tensing Norbu Norgay, one of the first men to climb Mount Everest was originally named "Namgyal Wangdi" which means Tuesday son of Wangdi

[9] And Ozias begat Joatham; and Joatham begat Achaz; and Achaz begat Ezekias;

[10] And Ezekias begat Manasses; and Manasses begat Amon; and Amon begat Josias;

[11] And Josias begat Jechonias and his brethren, about the time they were carried away to Babylon:

[12] And after they were brought to Babylon, Jechonias begat Salathiel; and Salathiel begat Zorobabel;

[13] And Zorobabel begat Abiud; and Abiud begat Eliakim; and Eliakim begat Azor;

[14] And Azor begat Sadoc; and Sadoc begat Achim; and Achim begat Eliud;

[15] And Eliud begat Eleazar; and Eleazar begat Matthan; and Matthan begat Jacob;

[16] And Jacob begat Joseph the husband of Mary, of whom was born Jesus, who is called Christ.

[17] So all the generations from Abraham to David are fourteen generations; and from David until the carrying away into Babylon are fourteen generations; and from the carrying away into Babylon unto Christ are fourteen generations.

The Jews of Biblical times were known by their family name and by their lineage. These two identifiers were very effective at that time in the world.

The population sizes allowed this. Names went far beyond identifiers. In ancient thought, a name was much more than just a means of distinguishing one person from another. It was in particular a means of revealing the inner being, the true nature of that person[24].

Genesis 25:26
KJV

---

[24] O'Brien, Peter T.; The Letter To The Ephesians. Grand Rapids, MI. Wm B. Eerdmans Publishing Co. pg. 256

[26] And after that came his brother out, and his hand took hold on Esau's heel; and his name was called Jacob: and Isaac was threescore years old when she bare them.

I Samuel 25:25
KJV
[25] Let not my lord, I pray thee, regard this man of Belial, even Nabal: for as his name is, so is he; Nabal is his name, and folly is with him: but I, thine handmaid, saw not the young men of my lord, whom thou didst send.

For God to give a name to a creature signifies His bringing them into existence, and exercising dominion over them. This also signifies the role that God gave them in the whole view of Creation. The name shows their significance and dependence upon Him. God's authority and power are stressed in these names both in heaven and on Earth[25].

Remember that the first service of man to God was the naming of the animals. Man received Revelation from God and named each animal signifying its position in the whole scheme of the creation.

Genesis 3:14
KJV
[14] And the LORD God said unto the serpent, Because thou hast done this, thou art cursed above all cattle, and above every beast of the field; upon thy belly shalt thou go, and dust shalt thou eat all the days of thy life:

God was the one who put the serpent (snake) as the lowest creature of the creation. It was cursed from that point on, all the way until the Revelation period. The name carries all the way through showing his "inner self" and it also acts as an identifier.

---

[25] Ibid.

Revelation 12:9,14,15
KJV
[9] And the great dragon was cast out, that old **serpent**, called the Devil, and Satan, which deceiveth the whole world: he was cast out into the earth, and his angels were cast out with him.
[14] And to the woman were given two wings of a great eagle, that she might fly into the wilderness, into her place, where she is nourished for a time, and times, and half a time, from the face of the **serpent**.
[15] And the **serpent** cast out of his mouth water as a flood after the woman, that he might cause her to be carried away of the flood.

Revelation 20:2
KJV
[2] And he laid hold on the dragon, that old **serpent**, which is the Devil, and Satan, and bound him a thousand years,

A name carries with it either strength or weakness. When the prophets spoke in God's name, God performed.

Deuteronomy 18:19,20
KJV
19] And it shall come to pass, that whosoever will not hearken unto my words which he shall speak **in my name**, I will require it of him.
[20] But the prophet, which shall presume to speak a word **in my name**, which I have not commanded him to speak, or that shall speak in the name of other gods, even that prophet shall die.

Mark 16:17,18
KJV
[17] And these signs shall follow them that believe; In my name shall they cast out devils; they shall speak with new tongues;
[18] They shall take up serpents; and if they drink any deadly thing, it shall not hurt them; they shall lay hands on the sick, and they shall recover.

These verses in Mark demonstrate the strength that is in the name of the Lord Jesus Christ. The verse is presenting healing, speaking in tongues which came with the new birth on the day of Pentecost, dominion, protection, and the ability to heal others.

Hence the Expanded Translation of the verse is rendered as follows:

Ephesians 3:15
Expanded Translation
[15] For whom the whole family, both on the Earth and in the Heavenlies is named.

Ephesians 3:16

This verse starts the intercessions by Paul to the Father on behalf of the saints. This is also the beginning of the first intercessory petition. As stated earlier there are three basic petitions in this section.

Three Reasonings of Intercessory Prayer

1. To be strengthened with might
2. By His spirit
3. In the inner man (In the heart of the man)

At the core of this first intercessory petition Paul requests power for the believers. He had already prayed that they know God and his incomprehensible might and power. Now he prays for them to be strengthened with might by His spirit in the inner man. This is not a militaristic power, or a physical strengthening.

> Ephesians 3:16
> KJV
> [16] That he would grant you, according to the riches of his glory, to be strengthened with might by his Spirit in the inner man;

> Ephesians 3:16
> RSV
> [16] that according to the riches of his glory he may grant you to be strengthened with might through his Spirit in the inner man,

Ephesians 3:16
NIV
[16] I pray that out of his glorious riches he may strengthen you with power through his Spirit in your inner being,

Ephesians 3:16
Aramaic Peshitta Version
[16] that he would allow you, according to the wealth of his glory, to be strengthened with power by his Rukha[26], that in your inner man.

Ephesians 3:16
Darby
[16] in order that he may give you according to the riches of his glory, to be strengthened with power by his Spirit in the inner man;

Paul's petition to God was a request to bring the greatness of God's power in fruition in their lives. What God is able to do in fulfillment of this petition is limitless. The riches of God's glory are beyond man's scope. In the prayer earlier in Ephesians 1:18 the believers are taken as God's inheritance, therefore they share in the vast riches of His glory. Paul understood that God had limitless resources in order to fulfill his requests so he came confidently before God in prayer.

Each of the beginnings of the English versions has a different translation to start the intercessory petition
Petitions:

1. KJV: That he would grant you
2. NIV: I pray that out of
3. APV: That he would allow you
4. YNG: That he may give you[27]

---

26 Rukha=spirit.
27 YNG= Youngs Literal Translation

5. MSG: I ask him to[28]In Response:
6. DAR: In order that he
7. RSV: That according to

These point to two different things. 1. Petitions 2. In response to. A petition is a genuine request to God, while setting this section as a response makes the granting of the petitions a sure, automatic sequential action. The evidence is clear that this prayer is an intercessory petition to God.

> Ephesians 1:13
> KJV
> [13] In whom ye also trusted, after that ye heard the word of truth, the gospel of your salvation: in whom also after that ye believed, ye were sealed with that holy spirit of promise,

> Ephesians 1:13
> RSV
> [13] In him you also, who have heard the word of truth, the gospel of your salvation, and have believed in him, were sealed with the promised Holy Spirit,

All the blessings of God that are spoken of in Ephesians were sealed to us by the Holy Spirit when we believed. In 1:13 we became sealed with all the blessings of the Father. Not "after" in the Greek reads literally "In whom, ye also, on believing were sealed" they are both aorist participles and mean literally either, *on hearing...* and *on believing* or *when ye* and *when ye believed.*[29]

Πλοῦτος (riches) derives its etymology from the Indo-Europ root "πελ" which means "to flow". The original meaning was taken to connote the act of "to fill". From this the Greek brings with it a sense of the fulness of

---

28 MSG= The Message
29 Bullinger, E.W.; The Prayers of Ephesians: Decatur, MI Invictus. No Copyright.

goods. They are the benefits of a happy life, lived within the parameters of the social order and standing within the blessings of the gods.

Homer uses the word as a state of life in which no work is required. In Homer's "Hesiod" he points to the idea that wealth is through work and work is honorable, not shameful. He develops the idea that only riches will bring blessings and virtue and that poverty is the realm of the sluggard and frays the nerves on this life.

> Psalm 73:12
> KJV
> [12] Behold, these are the ungodly, who prosper in the world; they increase in riches.

Aristotle believed that wealth was always within the material while Plato expounded the idea that wealth crossed both the realms of the spiritual and the material. Plato also made a distinction between the material riches of man and the true riches, which consisted of wisdom, virtue and culture.

The Stoics rejected the whole idea of the gathering of riches with their concept of "take for today for tomorrow may not appear, eat drink and be merry for tomorrow death may take us". Keeping riches and the pursuit of riches makes a man dependent upon things and relations so that he does not rest upon the only true support, namely himself. The Stoics' philosophy was foundational of the self-help principle.

Homer criticized the arrogance of the wealthy noble who looked down on the laboring peasant. Wealth and work, or individual conduct is so intertwined that we begin to see the development of the position where social status and net worth are no longer coincidental. Homer also noted that experience showed that there were poor who were cultured and uncultured who were rich. This disproved the notion that riches are the defining element of social stature[30].

---

[30] Kittel, Gerhard: Theological Dictionary Of The New Testament. Grand Rapids, MI. Wm. B. Eerdmans Publishing Company. 1964, Volume 6:319,320,322

When considering God's riches we see that His riches are beyond accounting. We also see that His riches envelop both the material and the spiritual realms.

> Psalm 104:24
> KJV
> [24] O LORD, how manifold are thy works! In wisdom hast thou made them all: the earth is full of thy riches.

> Romans 11:33
> KJV
> [33] O the depth of the riches both of the wisdom and knowledge of God! how unsearchable are his judgments, and his ways past finding out!

Kittel begins the definition of δοζα with an outline of an age old problem in the defining of this word "The historical problem in relation to this word-group is that in the biblical usage of the LXX and NT of the verb δοκέω more or less fully maintains the general Greek sense with no development in content, whereas there is significant change in the meaning of the noun, which both loses part of its secular sense in biblical Greek and also takes on an alien and specifically religious meaning shared, shared by the verb δοζάζω rather than δοκέω.[31]"

> I Corinthians 2:14
> KJV
> [14] But the natural man receiveth not the things of the Spirit of God: for they are foolishness unto him: neither can he know them, because they are spiritually discerned.

δοζα is one of very few words that transcends the spiritual into the physical realm that accurately describes an aspect of the spiritual. There are three separate and distinct parts that make up glory: radiance,

---

[31] Kittel, Gerhard: Theological Dictionary Of The New Testament. Grand Rapids, MI. Wm. B. Eerdmans Publishing Company. 1964, Vol II pg. 232.

reputation, and riches. The chief aspect of δοζα is radiance or light, it brings with it the idea of revealing or showing.

> I John 1:5
> KJV
> [5] This then is the message which we have heard of him, and declare unto you, that God is light, and in him is no darkness at all.

Light is seen in the physical realm, it has been analyzed and quantified. At the same time it is descriptive of the spiritual realm.

In non-biblical Greek δοζα has been used by Homer and Philo to mean "what one thinks" or "what one thinks of me[32]". This is in line with the definition of the verb δοκεω which means the same. In the noun form it is defined in part as "reputation". The concepts of δοζα being both light, which is visible in the physical, and "reputation" which is a conscience idea of the mortal man fits very well in the definition of the word.

"Riches of His glory" is a genitive of content meaning that the riches are an inherent part of the glory. However the true riches of glory are not static or hoarded but rather dynamic in nature. They are made available by patronage to those who request. This is the third part of glory. There is also an Anthropopathia figure of speech used here[33]. Riches are a human characteristic attributed to God. When the natural man thinks of riches, he thinks of gold, silver, very illuminated, a pot of gold at the end of the rainbow. However, God's riches are not in the physical realm.

> Psalm 24:1
> KJV
> [1] The **earth is the** LORD's, and the fulness thereof; the world, and they that dwell therein.

---

[32] Ibid pg. 234
[33] Bullinger, E.W.; Figures of Speech Used In The Bible, Ann Arbor Michigan, Baker Book House Company pg. 893

In Philo's "The Special Laws" or "A Treatise on Circumcision" Moses is said to have the following conversation with God.

> "I am persuaded by thy explanations that I should not have been able to receive the visible appearance of thy form. But I beseech thee that I may, at all events, behold the glory that is around thee. And I look upon thy glory to be the powers which attend thee as thy guards, the comprehension of which having escaped me up to the present time, worketh in me no slight desire of a thorough understanding of it." (46) But God replied and said, "The powers which you seek to behold are altogether invisible, and appreciable only by the intellect; since I myself am invisible and only appreciable by the intellect. And what I call appreciable only by the intellect are not those which are already comprehended by the mind, but those which, even if they could be so comprehended, are still such that the outward senses could not at all attain to them, but only the very purest intellect.[34]"

"To be strengthened with might by his spirit in the inner man" is not in regards to physical, or militaristic strength (as discussed in Ephesians 6). This phrase brings in the practical treatises. The words "by his spirit" is in reference to the gift of holy spirit the Christian receives when he believes and acts according to Romans 10:9,10. One need not look very far to understand being strengthened with might by his spirit in the inner man.

> Philippians 4:13
> KJV
> [13] I can do all things through Christ which strengtheneth

> Mark 11:23
> KJV
> [23] For verily I say unto you, That whosoever shall say unto this mountain, Be thou removed, and be thou cast

---

[34] Philo, The Special Laws I 45.

into the sea; and shall not doubt in his heart, but shall believe that those things which he saith shall come to pass; he shall have whatsoever he saith.

Strengthened – κραταιόω from the root κρατος is more closely related to ισχυς than to δυναμις therefore it denotes the presence and significance of force or strength than he exercise of it[35]. This is a might, or strength as a natural attribute. It connotes that the power or strength is present but not necessarily being demonstrated.

Paul very often would supply redundant adjectives or nouns throughout his letters. The addition of δύναμις in the dative is such a redundancy. The statement could easily stand without is, reading, "to be strengthened by his spirit in the inner man"

Paul specifies the type of power he is requesting on behalf of the believers. He is not asking for physical or militaristic forms of power. The Old Testament describes power in a physical manner as without holy spirit the Old Testament believer could not understand spiritual matters. To demonstrate the OT power we can begin with Samson.

> Judges 15:4
> KJV
> [4] And **Samson** went and caught three hundred foxes, and took firebrands, and turned tail to tail, and put a firebrand in the midst between two tails.

> Judges 16:3
> KJV
> [3] And **Samson** lay till midnight, and arose at midnight, and took the doors of the gate of the city, and the two posts, and went away with them, bar and all, and put them upon his shoulders, and carried them up to the top of an hill that is before Hebron.

---

[35] Kittel, Gerhard: Theological Dictionary Of The New Testament. Grand Rapids, MI. Wm. B. Eerdmans Publishing Company. 1964, Volume III pg. 905

Judges 16:25ff
KJV
[25] And it came to pass, when their hearts were merry, that they said, Call for **Samson**, that he may make us sport. And they called between the pillars.

[26] And **Samson** said unto the lad that held him by the hand, Suffer me that I may feel the pillars whereupon the house standeth, that I may lean upon them.

[27] Now the house was full of men and women; and all the lords of the Philistines were there; and there were upon the roof about three thousand men and women, that beheld while **Samson** made sport.

[28] And **Samson** called unto the LORD, and said, O Lord GOD, remember me, I pray thee, and strengthen me, I pray thee, only this once, O God, that I may be at once avenged of the Philistines for my two eyes.

[29] And **Samson** took hold of the two middle pillars upon which the house stood, and on which it was borne up, of the one with his right hand, and of the other with his left.

[30] And **Samson** said, Let me die with the Philistines. And he bowed himself with all his might; and the house fell upon the lords, and upon all the people that were therein. So the dead which he slew at his death were more than they which he slew in his life.

In Psalms, the Psalmist requested for the Children of Israel to become stronger than their enemies.

Psalm 105:4,24
KJV
[4] Seek the LORD, and his strength: seek his face evermore.

[24] And he increased his people greatly; and made them stronger than their enemies.

We also see God empowering individuals for specific tasks, such as Saul and Jonathan became stronger than lions.

> II Samuel 1:23
> KJV
> [23] Saul and Jonathan were lovely and pleasant in their
> lives, and in their death they were not divided: they were
> swifter than eagles, they were stronger than lions.

These are examples of God empowering his people for the tasks that they would face. Of course, they could only have understood power in a physical manner. They could never have been strengthened with might in the inner man. This was just not available to them

Homer's Iliad presents this as the strength or ability a man has inherent within. The strength is always in a state of either partial or full use. It is a view of the quantitative power present within the man. It is never to be considered necessarily as a demonstration of power. Used in a militaristic sense it means "to take by storm", again it is not a demonstration of the power by rather the ability of the army to "take by storm".

Κράτοζ almost always denotes the legal and valid superior power which connotes supremacy, and legally, politically, and physically that which turns the scales in one's favor[36]. With a genitive it takes a sense of power and control over something. This by nature brings the sense of supremacy and impending victory. Κράτοζ is not used of healing power nor is it descriptive of spirit beings[37]. κραταιόω outside of the Bible is only found in Philo[38].

The resources available to fulfill this confident request are limitless. They are (Lit) according to the riches of His glory. An expression

---

[36] Ibid

[37] This is never used in relation to the angels. See Hebrews 1&2

[38] Borgen, Peder., Fuglseth, Kare., and Skarsten, Roald.: The Philo Index; Grand Rapids, MI. Wm. B. Eerdmans Publishing Co. see Pg. 199

similar to this one is used in the earlier prayer where the readers, who are God's own inheritance, share in the riches of His glory.

The reference in Mark 11 is interesting in that Jesus is not referring to an actual mountain, as is the common teaching. There would be no need to remove the mountains in the area. Instead, Jesus is referring to a mountain of trash that Herod made in the area from his building projects. It was very unsightly to the inhabitants of Jerusalem and they would have wanted nothing more than to be rid of that huge mound of trash known as "Herod's Mountain". Though Jesus was present with them none of his followers attempted it. This demonstrated the need to be "strengthened with might by his spirit in the inner man".

The manifestation of faith must also be considered in any discussion of Ephesians 3:16.

> I Corinthians 12:7-11
> KJV
> [7] But the manifestation of the Spirit is given to every man to profit withal.
> [8] For to one is given by the Spirit the word of wisdom; to another the word of knowledge by the same Spirit;
> [9] To another faith by the same Spirit; to another the gifts of healing by the same Spirit;
> [10] To another the working of miracles; to another prophecy; to another discerning of spirits; to another divers kinds of tongues; to another the interpretation of tongues:
> [11] But all these worketh that one and the selfsame Spirit, dividing to every man severally as he will.

Verse 9 brings up the manifestation[39] of Faith. This is set as the power source of all of the other manifestations of holy spirit[40]. This manifestation of Faith is the ability with the help and guidance of the Holy Spirit to believe as Jesus Christ believed, thereby energizing the other manifestation that the man wills to operate. The power of the ability to believe as Jesus Christ could, demonstrated a strength that no man without the gift of the holy spirit within could ever emulate. This kind of Bible Faith[41] is still available today.

Paul's writing very frequently combined strength and love into one as he does so in this prayer. "To be strengthened with might by his spirit in the inner man, that Christ may dwell in your hearts by believing, that ye being rooted and grounded in love".

The "inner self" or the "inner being" requires an everyday renewal. This is accomplished of course by the Christian walk and the working of the Holy Spirit. This verse is working under the assumption that the believer as an individual is mature and acting as a member of the one body. The "inner self" is distinctly different from "the new man" in this regard. The "inner self" refers to the individual while the "new man" refers to the body of Christ as discussed in the previous doctrinal sections of Ephesians[42]. The renewing of the inner self is analogous with the building up of the body of Christ.

---

[39] These are often called gifts of the spirit however, manifestations is the closest associated noun to them and not the word "gifts". There is technically one gift to all the believers in Christ and that is the gift of holy spirit. Manifestations are the operations of the "gift".

[40] Reference here is to the gift of holy spirit within the individual believer, not God who is the Holy Spirit.

[41] There are several different kinds of faith talked about in the Scriptures. 1. The believing to salvation. 2. The believing of the Old Testament believers with the holy spirit upon but not dwelling within. 3. The faith of Jesus Christ and the ability granted by God to believers to energize the believing inherent in the gift of holy spirit. 4. the faith of the New Testament believers with the holy spirit within (internal) them.

[42] See Ephesians 4:24 and Colossians 3:9,10.

Ephesians 4:12
KJV
[12] For the perfecting of the saints, for the work of the
ministry, for the edifying of the body of Christ:

Paul uses inner man (εσο ανθροποζ) only two other times, Romans
7:22 where it appears to be the equivalent of "in the mind"[43], and also
II Corinthians 4:16 where Paul draws an analogy of the outward man
(materialistic and physical) and the inward man (non-material and
spiritual nature). "In the inner man" encompasses moral reasoning,
strength of moral fiber and of course the whole spiritual essence within
man[44].

The Expanded Translation for this verse is as follows:

Ephesians 3:16
Expanded Version
[16] That the Father of us all, will give unto you, in
accordance with the unquantifiable riches of His glory,
strength, with his great might, by his gift of holy spirit
in your innermost being

---

[43] See Romans 7:23,25
[44] This is not "holy spirit" within man but rather the alignment of the thoughts
and heart of man with holy spirit within. This is God's spirit working within man.

Ephesians 3:17

Ephesians 3:17
KJV
[17] That Christ may dwell in your hearts by faith; that ye, being rooted and grounded in love,

Ephesians 3:17
Revised Standard Version
[17] and that Christ may dwell in your hearts through faith; that you, being rooted and grounded in love,

Ephesians 3:17
New International Version
[17] so that Christ may dwell in your hearts through faith. And I pray that you, being rooted and established in love,

Ephesians 3:17
Aramaic Peshitta
[17] Meshikha would dwell in faith and in your hearts in love, as your root and your foundation becomes strong,

Ephesians 3:17
Darby
[17] that the Christ may dwell, through faith, in your hearts, being rooted and founded in love,

κατaοικῆσαι τόν χριστον – That Christ may dwell- This statement begins with the idea that it is connected to the previous verse. Since Paul's style of writing was such that the prayer is just one long sentence, the question arises, does this infinitive belong with the previous clause?

It could read "that God may grant that Christ may dwell in your hearts". If the clause is actually dependent upon κραταιωθῆναι it would properly read as "that God would grant you to be strengthened in the inner man so that, thus strengthened, Christ may dwell in your hearts".

Paul was not praying for the initial in-dwelling of Christ in their hearts. That had already occurred when they became born-again of God's Spirit. What Paul is petitioning of the Lord was for the continual presence of Christ in their hearts. This also was the prayer for the continual indwelling of God's spirit in their hearts

> Colossians 1:19
> RSV
> [19] For in him all the fulness of God was pleased to dwell,

> Colossians 2:9
> KJV
> [9] For in him dwelleth all the fulness of the Godhead bodily.

> Colossians 2:9
> RSV
> [9] For in him the whole fulness of deity dwells bodily,

This appears to be a separate petition, giving specialty and emphasis to the first petition of "to be strengthened with might"[45]. The whole idea of the petition "that Christ may dwell in your hearts by believing" is to show the intimate relationship we have with the Son of God and the permanence of his residence, which is within each Christian.

The verse connotes one of two things. It is either a declaration of the meaning of the previous verse, or it is another petition, a further intercessory request. The absence of a connecting conjunction between verse 16 & 17

---

[45] Calvin, Theophylact, and Zanchius held this position.

puts doubt upon the idea of this being a definition of the previous verse[46]. It can very well be stated that the presence of the indwelling Christ is a causal agent of the strengthening with might by his spirit in the inner man.

In order to express what is necessary for the understanding of the love of Christ two metaphors are utilized, one botanical and one architectural - "rooted" and "founded". A double metaphor is a rare occasion and serves as a figure of speech calling attention to itself. This calls an importance to this verse.

Paul could not pray that Christ would dwell in one's heart, for from the moment of the new birth his residence is established. Any prayer concerning the gift of holy spirit in a believer can only be the enlargement of what indwelling and the ability to utilize further what it is capable of. What Paul is requesting is a realization of the presence and capabilities of the gift within.

The Syriac version, along with some of the Greek Fathers and some Latin commentaries[47]join the two clauses together, "in order that Christ may inhabit the inner man by faith which is in your hearts". However, the reader must realize that for every opinion or idea there are always those that are in opposition to it. In this instance Harless and Calvin believed that the statement keeps verse 16 reading as "to be strengthened with might by his spirit in the inner man".

This phrase was shocking to the ancient world as the idea of gods actually living among the men was unheard of. Artemis was the primary goddess worshipped in Ephesus, Zeus was worshipped in Laodicea. In fact, Laodicea was known as the city of Zeus. However, these gods did not live among or in the people. Their home was believed to be on top of Mt. Olympus in Greece. To think of the gods living and communing with the common people was absolutely wrong, and to teach such a thing was considered a heresy. In Rome the Pantheon was built to be a common home for the gods of Rome.

---

[46] Longman, Tremper III and Garland, David E.: The Expositor's Bible Commentary Revised Edition, Ephesians – Philemon, Grand Rapids, MI pg98
[47] Ambroister and Pelagius

The Epistle to the Romans is addressed to the individual, bringing him from death unto life. It shows him or her their state as Christians, bringing them to be rooted in their state and standing in the Lord. Ephesians is the Individual in the family of God and their state and standing as a member of the family of God, founded into a holy temple in the Lord. Thus the verse reads "rooted and founded in love".

The phrase "That ye being rooted and grounded in love" is oftentimes considered to be a part of verse 18. This is a good demonstration of the shortcomings of the location system of verse delineation. If the phrase is part of verse 18 it would read "ye have been rooted and grounded in love in order that".

The second part of this verse is a Parembole or Insertion, which is a figure of speech. It is a parenthetic addition of information that is capable of standing on its own. A Parembole can be totally an independent addition of information relevant to the topic, yet the topic can stand without the information. E.W. Bullinger states that Ephesians 3:2-13 is a Parembole all its own[48]. This Parembole brings further information to the prayer. "Being rooted and grounded in love" pulls in two more analogies to the body. This figure brings in the concepts of rooted as a tree and grounded or "founded" as a building. Rooted takes into account the individual as a child of God.

> Psalm 1:1-3
> KJV
> [1] Blessed is the man that walketh not in the counsel of the ungodly, nor
> [2] But his delight is in the law of the LORD; and in his law doth he meditate day and night.
> [3] And he shall be like a tree planted by the rivers of water, that bringeth forth his fruit in his season; his leaf also shall not wither; and whatsoever he doeth shall prosper.

---

[48] Bullinger, E.W.; Figures of Speech Used In The Bible, Ann Arbor Michigan, Baker Book House Company pg476

Also note Colossians 2:7 which is a parallel statement to Ephesians 3:17. Once again both a botanical and an architectural analogy is utilized here.

> Colossians 2:6,7
> KJV
> [6] As ye have therefore received Christ Jesus the Lord, so walk ye in him:
> [7] Rooted and built up in him, and stablished in the faith, as ye have been taught, abounding therein with thanksgiving.

Both of these sections concern themselves with the individual in Christ, strong in the faith, steadfast and unmovable[49].

Grounded as a building takes in the thought of the individual as a part of the family. Consider the "G" section of the doctrinal treatises of the epistle[50]. To be grounded looks at the foundation of the building.

> Matthew 7:24ff
> KJV
> [24] Therefore whosoever heareth these sayings of mine, and doeth them, I will liken him unto a wise man, which built his house upon a rock:
> [25] And the rain descended, and the floods came, and the winds blew, and beat upon that house; and it fell not: for it was founded upon a rock.
> [26] And every one that heareth these sayings of mine, and doeth them not, shall be likened unto a foolish man, which built his house upon the sand:

---

[49] It is important to note that of the 11 uses of the word "rooted" all the uses of it in the LXX and the Apocrypha" and in the gospel talk about being "rooted out" It is not until we see in the Epistles that rooted means to have your roots firmly in place.

[50] See Appendix B

[27] And the rain descended, and the floods came, and the winds blew, and beat upon that house; and it fell: and great was the fall of it.

[28] And it came to pass, when Jesus had ended these sayings, the people were astonished at his doctrine:

[29] For he taught them as one having authority, and not as the scribes.

Colossians 1:23

KJV

[23] If ye continue in the faith grounded and settled, and be not moved away from the hope of the gospel, which ye have heard, and which was preached to every creature which is under heaven; whereof I Paul am made a minister;

Individuals grounded in the faith are required for the church to operate properly and for the church to be rooted in the faith. The consideration here is for both the individual and the church as a single entity.

While Paul derives some of his language from the Greek world concerning "inner man" his ideas here are not particularly Greek in their origin. Paul speaks here about the ability of the Christian believer to live a life of righteousness through the spirit. This points to certain verses in the Old Testament.

Psalm 119:11

KJV

[11] Thy word have I hid in mine heart, that I might not sin against thee.

Exodus 15:2

KJV

[2] The LORD is my strength and song, and he is become my salvation: he is my God, and I will prepare him an habitation; my father's God, and I will exalt him.

Jeremiah 16:19
KJV
[19] O LORD, my strength, and my fortress, and my refuge in the day of affliction, the Gentiles shall come unto thee from the ends of the earth, and shall say, Surely our fathers have inherited lies, vanity, and things wherein there is no profit.

Remembering that Figures of Speech are the Holy Spirits' marking drawing attention to what is important in the scriptures, there is another Ellipsis in verses 17,18 that begins at the end of Verse 17. It is an Ellipsis: Absolute of the Pronoun[51]. Love is referred to in this verse but is absent in the next verse.

Ephesians 3:17b
KJV
that ye being rooted and grounded in love

If we carry this through to the next verse, we see the Ellipsis. "may know the breadth (of love) and length (of love) and depth (of love) and height (of love) and to know the love of Christ. The immeasurable focus on love is nicely bracketed here with everything in between being supplied by the Ellipsis; Absolute of the Pronoun. The Expanded Translation of this verse is as follows:

Ephesians 3:17
Expanded Version
[17] So that Christ, The only begotten of the Father, will dwell in you hearts by the faith you have demonstrated; that you, who being rooted as a tree and founded as a building in love,

---

[51] Bullinger, E.W.; Figures of Speech Used In The Bible, Ann Arbor Michigan, Baker Book House Company 1968 pg18

Ephesians 3:18

The Great Prayer of Ephesians is filled with Figures of Speech that just go to show the importance of this section of scriptures. We find at least three different occurrences of an Ellipsis, and v18 is still one of the prime examples of this figure.

Ephesians 3:18
King James Version
[18] May be able to comprehend with all saints what is the breadth, and length, and depth, and height;

Ephesians 3:18
Revised Standard Version
[18] may have power to comprehend with all the saints what is the breadth and length and height and depth,

Ephesians 3:18
New International Version
[18] may have power, together with all the Lord's holy people, to grasp how wide and long and high and deep is the love of Christ,

Ephesians 3:18
Aramaic Peshitta Version
[18] that you would be able to understand with all the holy [ones] what is the height and depth and length and breadth

Ephesians 3:18
Tyndale Ploughboy New Testament

[18] moun comprehende with alle seyntis, which is
the breede and the lengthe and the hiynesse and the
depnesse

Ephesians 3: 18
Darby New Testament
[18] may be able to grasp (with all Christians) how wide
and deep and long and high is the love of Christ

"To comprehend or to grasp, be able to understand" is the word
Καταλαμβάνω. Κατα, means from above to below, it is a vertical line
meaning that the root of the comprehension has to be from God down
to the believer. λαμβάνω in the active means "to take or to bring under
ones control on ones own initiative"[52]. In its simplest form it really means
to "receive". In the language of Jurisprudence it means to receive a final
judgment of things to which one has a claim[53]. Passively it is to acquire.
God cannot receive anything (except praise, love and worship) because
He is the possessor of everything. The scriptures alone define His total
nature and character. λαμβάνω is a much stronger form of receiving than
δεχομαι, which is to receive objectively, for instance flowers, one usually
receives them and does nothing more than look at them. If you were
to λαμβάνω then you would cross-pollinate, collect seeds and replant
them. Καταλαμβάνω comes from above to be received below. The act
of the reception is an active one, the receiver must grasp, or overtake the
object. Philo uses the word "to grasp and truly understand"[54]. It also is
used of the Christian's crown of victory in I Corinthians.

I Corinthians 9:24
KJV
[24] Know ye not that they which run in a race run all,
but one receiveth the prize? So run, that ye may obtain.

---

[52] Kittel, Gerhard: Theological Dictionary Of The New Testament. Grand
Rapids, MI. Wm. B. Eerdmans Publishing Company. 1964, Vol IV pg. 5
[53] Ibid
[54] Philo Praem Poen 490

I Corinthians 9:24,25
Darby
[24] Know ye not that they who run in the race run all,
but one receives the prize? Thus run in order that ye
may obtain.
[25] But everyone that contends for a prize is temperate
in all things: they then indeed that they may receive a
corruptible crown, but we an incorruptible.

Looking back at the chart regarding the Prayer we see that the
Introversion aspects of the chart (prayer) line up v16 with v18

A. To be granted according to the riches of His grace Eph 3:16

A. To comprehend with all saints Eph 3:18

Any discussion about comprehension or Καταλαμβάνω requires that
we look at Acts 4.

Acts 4:13
KJV
[13] Now when they saw the boldness of Peter and John,
and perceived that they were unlearned and ignorant
men, they marvelled; and they took knowledge of them,
that they had been with Jesus.

This knowledge that they demonstrated could only have come from
God. They had grasped fundamentally the word of God. As discussed
in Ephesians 3:18, God made available to all believers the all-permeating
truth and greatness of the ἀγάπε του χριστου. A requirement of the
receipt of this comprehension is that it must be refreshed in the believer
each day in the life of faith until it is finally consummated at the
resurrection[55].

---

[55] Kittel, Gerhard: Theological Dictionary Of The New Testament. Grand
Rapids, MI. Wm. B. Eerdmans Publishing Company. 1964, Vol IV pg. 10

Καταλαμβάνω is a colorful way of expressing the comprehension. The word is also translated "possessed", "to take" amongst other English words in the Old Testament. It is used in Joshua

> Joshua 19:47
> KJV
> [47] And the coast of the children of Dan went out too little for them: therefore the children of Dan went up to fight against Leshem, and took it, and smote it with the edge of the sword, and possessed it (Καταλαμβάνω), and dwelt therein, and called Leshem, Dan, after the name of Dan their father.

> Joshua 8:19
> KJV
> [19] And the ambush arose quickly out of their place, and they ran as soon as `he had stretched out his hand: and they entered into the city, and took it (Καταλαμβάνω), and hasted and set the city on fire.

We also see Καταλαμβάνω in the book of Acts when God gave Peter a vision of a sheet coming down from heaven.

> Acts 10:9-16
> KJV
> [9] On the morrow, as they went on their journey, and drew nigh unto the city, Peter went up upon the housetop to pray about the sixth hour:
> [10] And he became very hungry, and would have eaten: but while they made ready, he fell into a trance,
> [11] And saw heaven opened, and a certain vessel descending unto him, as it had been a great sheet knit at the four corners, and let down to the earth:
> [12] Wherein were all manner of four-footed beasts of the earth, and wild beasts, and creeping things, and fowls of the air.

[13] And there came a voice to him, Rise, Peter; kill, and eat.

[14] But Peter said, Not so, Lord; for I have never eaten anything that is common or unclean.

[15] And the voice spake unto him again the second time, What God hath cleansed, that call not thou common.

[16] This was done thrice: and the vessel was received up again into heave

It seems that all English version agree on the use of four-dimensions, which occur in our three-dimensional world. The Ephesians were familiar with this phraseology as it was used with variable frequency in the cultic religions. It is not like Paul to import phrases from the cultic in order to bring understanding to the reader from sources they were used too. In the [56] PGM IV 975-985 (Greek Magical Papyri) it is used as follows:

Spell: "I conjure you, holy light, holy brightness, breadth, depth, length, height, brightness, by the holy names *I* which I have spoken and am now going to speak. By ΙΑδ ΣΑΒΑδΤΗ ΑΡΒΑΤΗΙΑδ ΣΕΣΕΝΓΕΝΒΑΡΠΗΑΡΑΓΓΕΣ ΑΒΛΑΝΑΤΗΑΝΑΛΒΑ ΑΚ– ΡΑΜΜΑΞΗΑΜΑΙΥ ΑΙ ΑΙ ΙΑΟ ΑΧ ΑΧ ΙΝΑΧ, remain by me in the present hour, until I pray to the god / and learn about the things I desire. Give me your strength, Give me your might."

Light Retaining Spell that is spoken once *I* in order that the light-magic might remain with you, for sometimes when you invoke the god-bringing spell darkness is produced. Therefore, you should conjure in the following way

Spell: "I conjure you, holy light, holy brightness, breadth, depth, length, height, brightness, by the holy names *I* which I have spoken and am now going to speak. remain by me in the present

---

[56] A special thank you to Hans dieter Betz for his translation of the passage and for allowing me to use these two quotations. The Greek Magical Papyri in Translation Including The Demotic Spells.

FRANK ABISSI JR. TH.D., PH.D.

hour, until I pray to the god / and 1 earn about the things I desire.»

It is found in another magical incantation in PGM IV 955-970. as another aspect of light:

> *Light bringing Spell:* Crown your head with the same spray): stand in the same fashion facing the lamp, close your eyes and recite this spell 7 times.

> *Spell:* "I call upon you, the living god, *I* fiery, invisible begetter of light, ΙΑΕΛ ΠΙΕΤΑ ΠΗΟΣ ΖΑ ΠΑΙ ΠΗΤΗΕΝΤΗΑ ΠΗΟΣΖΑ ΠΨΡΙ ΒΕΛΙΑ ΙΑΟ ΙΑΟ ΕΨΟ ΟΕΕ Α ΟΨ ΕΟΙ Α Ε Ε ΙΟ Ψ Ο give your strength, rouse your daimon, *I* enter into this fire, fill it with a divine spirit, and show me your might. Let there be opened for me the house of the all-powerful god **ALBALAL**[57]," who is in this light. *I* Let there be light, breadth, depth, Length, height, brightness, and let him who is inside shine through, the lord [58]

When the person who was quoting these incantations wanted a greater insight into the deity he would repeat "Give me your strength, give me your might" as a petition to the god for a deeper wisdom and understanding. This idea is also found in the Prayer of Ephesians.

Paul very often used wording from the cultic as this is something the people really understood. This does not mean that what is in God's Word is cultic in any sense of the word (except back in the first three centuries after Christ, as Christianity was developing as a "religion" among so many others). The full intention of Paul was to pronounce the word in language that was easily understood by the people at the time. Since the cultic religions were all that the Ephesians knew before turning to Christianity, Paul wrote in phrases that were easily understood in regard to their religious life.

---

[57] Thought to be a continuation of Baal worship
[58] Betz, Hans Dieter.:The Greek Magical Papyri in Translation Including the Demotic Spells. Chicago and London, The University of Chicago Press Pg.57

I Corinthians 9:20-22

[20] And unto the Jews I became as a Jew, that I might gain the Jews; to them that are under the law, as under the law, that I might gain them that are (being not without law to God, but under the law to Christ,) that I might gain them that are without law.[22] To the weak became I as weak, that I might gain the weak: I am made all things to all men, that I might by all means save some.

Ephesians 3:18 presents as the terminus of one ellipses and part of another ellipsis. The first is discussed previously in the last paragraph Verse 17. There are four terms that should be examined here. Bengal talks in his Gnomon on the New Testament of these four dimensions:

The Four Dimensions

Breadth - Extending to all races, people of all nations.
Length - it spans ALL ages from everlasting to everlasting.
Depth - No creature can ascertained.
Height - No enemy can ascertain or reach[59]

No part of God's creation has these four things as a part of it. Consider the recent concept of the ever-expanding universe. The concept of the Big Bang Theory fits in very well with Genesis 1:1. In the beginning God put those two atoms in motion, hitting each other at the exact right time, place, speed, and angle for an explosion to take place that He could use to create the Heavens and the Earth. In no place does the Word of God say that the universe is complete. With the creation of many billions of stars and even more planets there is nothing that prohibits His making more of the universe.

---

[59] John Bengal Edited by Rev. W.L. Blackley M.A. and Rev. James Hawes, M.A. The Gnomon of the New Testament: London: Daldy, Isbister & Co 56 Ludgate Hill 1876

Bengal notes a figure of speech in the comparison of Ephesians 3:10,13 and verse 18 called a Chiasmus or a "cross reference[60]" The Latins called this figure a Decussata Oratio or to divide cross wise. In this case an alternation is developed by the figure.[61]; Bullinger describes a Chiaston (or Chiasmos) as two converging series the first of one series corresponds with the last of the second; the second of the first corresponds with the *penultimate* (or the last but one) of the second. And the third of the first corresponds with the *antepenultimate* of the second. This is to say there are at least six members. The first corresponds with the sixth the second with the fifth the third with the fourth and so on.

It is interesting to note that most theologians believe that all these measurements were physical, such as the measurements that a carpenter would make in his building of a structure. They fail to think that three of the measurements are physical which people relate to while the fourth is a measurement of time. This makes the measurement conceivable in man's understanding.

Introverted Correspondence

A. Love of Christ
    B. Breadth
        C. Love of Christ
            D. Length
            D. Love of Christ
        C. Depth
    B. Love of Christ
A. Height

---

[60] A chiasmus is a rhetorical literary figure of speech whose words, concepts and ideals are repeated in a reverse order in the same or a modified form to fit the structure, such as poetry.

[61] John Bengal Edited by Rev. W.L. Blackley M.A. and Rev. James Hawes, M.A.; The Critical English New Testament in Three Volumes: Commentary on the Entire New Testament, London: Daldy, Isbister & Co. 56 Ludgate Hill 1876

It is of note that the dimensions of the temple refer to all the fulness of God while the individual dimensions make reference to the love of Christ. Verse 19 is the appropriate response of the Church.

These dimensions of the spiritual temple refer to the fulness of God v19 to which the Church, according to the measure of its ability should correspond; Compare V10,13 on Christ for the breadth of the fulness and of the love of Christ is meant; and that in reference to all mankind and all people ; It's length all ages ; verse 21; It's depth no part of the creation can ascertain; it's height can no enemy attain, God's protection is very real. Compare Psalm 67. In comparison of breadth, length, depth and height which together comprise on magnitude, there is nothing broad, deep, (A Chiasmus is cross-reference]) between love, breadth, love, fulness. The third answers to the firsthand consequently the second to the fourth {Alternation) in the 19th verse is an expression of love; in the 18th of the fulness of God in itself; but this is imbued with love (But these are not dimensions of the spiritual temple to which there is no allusion, but of the love of Christ to men.).

E.W. Bullinger suggests an interesting rendering of Eph v17-19. "That Christ may dwell in your hearts through faith. That (ἵνα) ye, being rooted and grounded in love, may be strong to apprehend with all the saints what is the breadth and length and height and depth {of love is} even (te) to know the love of Christ which passeth knowledge" ff.[62] Depth always comes before height as the foundation of a building is dependent upon the depth of the foundation to hold the building up (height).

We will never be able to grasp or understand love in all its length, depth, breadth, and height until we experientially know Christ's love for us. It is so deep it is unfathomable, so high the summit cannot be reached. Its breadth extends beyond all borders. The length reaches from eternity to everlasting.

---

[62] Ibid

FRANK ABISSI JR. TH.D., PH.D.

This verse is the pinnacle of this prayer as noted in the structure presented in the beginning of this work. This presents to the Christian believer the fulness of the unsearchable riches of the love of God.

Job 5:8ff
KJV
[8] I would seek unto God, and unto God would I commit my cause:
[9] which doeth great things and unsearchable; marvellous things without number:
[10] who giveth rain upon the earth, and sendeth waters upon the fields:
[11] To set up on high those that be low; that those which mourn may be exalted to safety.
[12] He disappointeth the devices of the crafty, so that their hands cannot perform their enterprise.
[13] He taketh the wise in their own craftiness: and the counsel of the froward is carried headlong.
[14] They meet with darkness in the daytime, and grope in the noonday as in the night.
[15] But he saveth the poor from the sword, from their mouth, and from the hand of the mighty.
[16] So the poor hath hope, and iniquity stoppeth her mouth.
[17] Behold, happy is the man whom God correcteth: therefore despise not thou the chastening of the Almighty:
[18] for he maketh sore, and bindeth up: he woundeth, and his hands make whole.
[19] He shall deliver thee in six troubles: yea, in seven there shall no evil touch thee.
[20] In famine he shall redeem thee from death: and in war from the power of the sword.
[21] Thou shalt be hid from the scourge of the tongue: neither shalt thou be [22] At destruction and famine

thou shalt laugh: neither shalt thou be afraid of the beasts of the earth.

[23] For thou shalt be in league with the stones of the field: and the beasts of the field shall be at peace with thee.

[24] And thou shalt know that thy tabernacle shall be in peace; and thou shalt visit thy habitation, and shalt not sin.

[25] Thou shalt know also that thy seed shall be great, and thine offspring as the grass of the earth.

[26] Thou shalt come to thy grave in a full age, like as a shock of corn cometh in his season.

[27] Lo this, we have searched it, so it is; hear it, and know thou it for thy good.

Barach 3:18ff

[18] For they that wrought in silver, and were so careful, and whose works are **unsearchable**,

O Lord, Almighty God of our fathers, Abraham, Isaac, and Jacob, and of their righteous seed; who hast made heaven and earth, with all the ornament thereof; who hast bound the sea by the word of thy commandment; who hast shut up the deep, and sealed it by thy terrible and glorious name; whom all men fear, and tremble before thy power; for the majesty of thy glory cannot be borne, and thine angry threatening toward sinners is importable: but thy merciful promise is unmeasurable and **unsearchable**; for thou art the most high Lord, of great compassion, longsuffering, very merciful, and repentest of the evils of men. Thou, O Lord, according to thy great goodness hast promised repentance and forgiveness to them that have sinned against thee: and of thine infinite mercies hast appointed repentance unto sinners that they may be saved. Thou therefore, O Lord, that art the God of the just, hast not appointed repentance the just, as to Abraham, and Isaac, and Jacob, which have not sinned against thee; but thou hast appointed repentance unto me that am a sinner: for I have sinned above the number of the sands of the sea. My transgressions, O Lord, are multiplied: my transgressions are multiplied, and I am not worthy to behold and see the height of heaven for the multitude of mine iniquities. I am bowed down with many iron bands, that I cannot life up mine head, neither have any release: for I have provoked thy wrath and done evil before thee: I did not thy will, neither kept I thy commandments: I have set up abominations and have multiplied offences. Now therefore I bow the knee of mine heart, beseeching thee of grace. I have sinned, O Lord, I have sinned, and I acknowledge mine iniquities: wherefore, I humbly beseech thee, forgive me, O Lord, forgive me, and destroy me not with mine iniquites. Be not angry with me forever, by reserving evil for me; neither condemn me to the lower parts of the earth. For thou art the God, even the God of them that repent; and in me thou wilt shew all thy goodness: for thou wilt save me that am unworthy, according to thy great mercy. Therefore I will praise thee forever all the days \of my life: for all the powers of the heavens do praise thee, and thine is the glory forever and ever. Amen[63].

It is important to realize that what is talked about here is NOT the actual love of Christ. It is a partial description of some of the characteristics of the love of Christ.

Looking at πλάτος we find that it is used only three times in the Greek New Testament. It is used here in Ephesians, then in Revelation.

Revelation 20:9
KJV
[9] And they went up on the breadth of the earth, and compassed the camp of the saints about, and the beloved

---

[63] Though not a universally accepted part of the cannon Baruch and other Apocryphal writing add to the definitions of the Word of God. They may or may not be God-Breathed. In some instances they are the only other use of a word in biblical usage.

city: and fire came down from God out of heaven, and
devoured them.

Revelation 21:16-21
KJV
[16] And the city lieth foursquare, and the length is
as large as the breadth: and he measured the city with
the reed, twelve thousand furlongs. The length and the
breadth and the height of it are equal.
[17] And he measured the wall thereof, an hundred and
forty and four cubits, according to the measure of a man,
that is, of the angel.
[18] And the building of the wall of it was of jasper: and
the city was pure gold, like unto clear glass.
[19] And the foundations of the wall of the city were
garnished with all manner of precious stones. The first
foundation was jasper; the second, sapphire; the third,
a chalcedony; the fourth, an emerald;
[20] The fifth, sardonyx; the sixth, sardius; the seventh,
chrysolite; the eighth, beryl; the ninth, a topaz; the
tenth, a chrysoprasus; the eleventh, a jacinth; the
twelfth, an amethyst.
[21] And the twelve gates were twelve pearls; every
several gate was of one pearl: and the street of the city
was pure gold, as it were transparent glass.

πλατύνο which is related to πλάτος and helps define this word.

Matthew 23:5
KJV
[5] But all their works they do for to be seen of men:
they make broad their phylacteries, and enlarge the
borders of their garments,

Phylacteries were small boxes that were attached to the forehead with
two thin leather straps. Inside these boxes were small papyri upon which

scriptures were written that pertained to the life of the person at the time they wore them. This way the Word of God was always before them as they were written on the tables of their heart.

> Proverbs 3:3
> KJV
> [3] Let not mercy and truth forsake thee: bind them about thy neck; write them upon the table of thine heart:

To make broad the phylacteries means to use a large, wide phylactery. This gave them the illusion of being more pious as though they were making more of an effort. It has nothing to say of whether the sincerity and believing was there. It was nothing more than a pose of advanced Piety.

Philo in his writings on sobriety says the following:

> Sobriety 61
> "(61) And she is said not to have had a mother, having received the inheritance of relationship from her father only, and not from her mother, having no share in the female race; for someone has said somewhere, "And yet, in truth, she is my sister, the daughter of my father, but not the daughter of my Mother."{14}{genesis 20:12.} For she is not formed of **the material perceptible by the outward senses,** which is always in a state of formation things; among which, first of all, the tree of wisdom sprang up, but rather of the cause and father of all. (62) She, therefore, having emerged out of the **whole corporeal world**, and exulting from the joy which is in God, laughs at the pursuits of men, which are conversant about either war or peace.[64]

---

[64] Philo Sobriety, line 61,62

On The Life Of Moses II.

(86) And of the forty which are included in the calculation and made up of the width of the ten curtains, the length takes thirty, for such is the length of the tabernacle, and the chamber **behind** takes nine. And the remaining one is in the outer vestibule, that it may be the bond to unite the whole circumference.[65]

So Philo uses the word pla?0toz instead of "breadth" as not being perceptible by the five senses of man, the material is so expansive, He describes the whole immeasurable corporeal world as descriptive of the "breadth". He uses four dimensions in the life of Moses. 1. The width of the ten curtains. 2. Such is the length of the tabernacle 3. The chamber "breadth" takes nine, 4. And the remaining one in the outer vestibule.

Βάθοϛ, translated as depth is used as an indistinct descriptor of both physical and spiritual things.

> Mark 4:5
> KJV
> [5] And some fell on stony ground, where it had not much earth; and immediately it sprang up, because it had no depth of earth:

Discussing depth of earth this particular usage is relevant to the quality and compactness of soil upon which the seed is sown. The foundation of the Temple had to be on good ground with depth. The first usage of a word sets the pattern for its translation throughout the Word of God. A section in Job works with three of these. This is the first usage also of Βάθοϛ

> Job 11:5-8
> KJV
> [5] But oh that God would speak, and open his lips against thee;

---

[65] Philo, II On the Life of Moses, line 86

[6] And that he would shew thee the secrets of wisdom, that they are double to that which is! Know therefore that God exacteth of thee less than thine iniquity deserveth.

[7] Canst thou by searching find out God? canst thou find out the Almighty unto perfection?

[8] It is as high as heaven; what canst thou do? deeper (Βάθος) than hell; what canst thou know?

[9] The measure thereof is longer than the earth, and broader than the sea.

The question of verse 7 cannot be answered in the affirmative. However, comparing this with Ephesians we see the following.

Job - Ephesians Comparison

Job 11:7-9	Ephesians 3:18
1. Inability to find out God	Comprehend with all saints
2. High as Heaven	No enemy can ascertain or reach
3. Deeper than Hell	No creature can ascertain
4. Broader than the Sea	Extending to all races, people of all
5. Longer than the Earth	It spans ALL ages, everlasting to everlasting

6. Βάθος according to Kittel's means an external depth, the depth of a stratum. It also provides a downward direction of travel. It does not suggest the depth of something. These two sections are "Anthropopathic as to State"[66] Figures of Speech, meaning that they attribute human characteristics to God who is Spirit. Spirit transcends height, depth, breadth, and length of time. None of these natural states of measure are applicable to the state of spirit, nor do they hold any consequence to spirit.

---

[66] Bullinger, E.W.; Figures of Speech Used In The Bible, Ann Arbor Michigan, Baker Book House Company pg. 871

Both of these sections of scriptures are also Idiomas[67] The language here is peculiar to the Jews, though the uses of the idiom are approximately 1700 years apart. Both of these sections are also considered "Idiomas of Elements" where 3 or more elements are used in a description of an Anthropopathic state. Figures of speech are not always exclusive of one another and at times are compounding.

> Ezekiel 31:5
> KJV
> [4] The waters made him great, the deep set him up on high with her rivers running round about his plants, and sent out her little rivers unto all the trees of the field.
> [5] Therefore his height was exalted above all the trees of the field, and his boughs were multiplied, and his branches became long because of the multitude of waters, when he shot forth.

Not identical however these two verses are similar to the Idioma of Job. Deep, high, height, and long.

μῆκος simply meaning length. It works in two different arenas, a physical measurement such as a meter. It is also used to define a portion (or whole) of time. Length, μηκος is only used two times in the Greek New Testament, yet many times in the LXX. Every usage of it in the Old Testament means a physical length. It is not used of time in the LXX. Looking a step forward μῆκος is the root of the word μηκύ nomai which in the Greek New Testament is used just one time.

> Mark 4:27
> KJV
> [27] And should sleep, and rise night and day, and the seed should spring and grow up (μηκύνομαι), he knoweth not how.

---

[67] Ibid pg. 819 Bullinger states there are three different circumstances any one of which defines an idioma. 1. Language peculiar to the vulgar as opposed to the classical 2. Language peculiar to one tribe or nation as opposed to other languages or dialects, 3. Language peculiar to any one particular author or speaker

Growing up has a point of termination. The seed "springing" denotes the actual act of growing, while to be "grown up" marks the end of the springing up cycle, the terminus. Here it represents a fixed, measurable point. ὕψος is extremely rare in usage outside of the scriptures. When it is used, it means "to lift up" or slightly more frequently as "to raise up".

Height seems to be a redundancy of depth. One measure is vertically up, while the other is vertically down. This gives the allusion that the love of Christ is in a cube shape. ὕψος can be a high place, a mountain top or summit, and also can be the highlands. It is taken to be a measurement of these places. In the classical Greek it is often times used to mean the "climax" of a speech, which is reached through the dynamics of words by the orator who can transcend himself[68]. In other instances, it is used of the sky in its violent fury of lightning and thunder, and tempest in order to bring out the divine aspect of ὕψος the rapture on high is what this is pointing towards. The immeasurable height of the third heaven extends upward as ὕψος.

Severin of Gabala[69] uses the four arms of the cross to demonstrate Christ crucified with the ὕψος extending up toward heaven and the Deity, while the Βάθος extending down into the deep towards Hades. The descent is also representative of the humanity of Jesus. Both the humiliation and the exaltation are seen here. The μῆκος and the πλάτος going east and west, spreading the Gospel all over the world.

The argument that comes with Severin of Gabala's writings is that Jesus Christ died not on a cross as we imagine it to be but rather a stake in the ground. This goes to beg the question "was the cross an actual Roman style cross or is it a metaphoric cross?" Since the Romans carried out the crucifixion it is most likely that an actual cross was used.

---

[68] Kittel, Gerhard: Theological Dictionary Of The New Testament. Grand Rapids, MI. Wm. B. Eerdmans Publishing Company. 1964, Vol VIII pg. 602

[69] Severian, Bishop of Gabala in Syria was a popular preacher in Constantinople from around 398/399 until 404. he worked with Empress Eudoxia He became the enemy of John Chrysostom and helped condemn him at the Synod of the Oak. A paraphrase of his "Discourse on the Seals" concerning the cannon of the Gospels is cited here.

Previously Theologians believed that the measurements spoken of here were in reference to the Ark of the Covenant. The prevalent thought among theologians now is that the four measurements here are significant of the Holy Temple of God. This may be so but, we need to consider each word and their significance and relationship to one another. Only in the divine setting can this verse be used to substantiate a relationship of the measurements, as three are physical and one (length) is a measure of time. All too often people seem to think that this is a special four quantifiable measurements of a sacra building in the Lord. Utilizing the fact that length is a measure of time makes this fact implausible. Time, like the other measurements can also be unquantifiable, reaching from eternal to everlasting. Breadth, depth, and height, can all be both quantifiable and unquantifiable. Over the years the measurements have been said to refer to:

Possible subjects of the four dimensions of Ephesians 3:18

1. The vastness of God's Power
2. The Love of Christ
3. The "Mystery" of God's plan
4. The Manifold wisdom of God
5. The New Temple
6. The Heavenly Inheritance. the New Jerusalem, thought of like a cube[70]
7. The four arms of the Cross which embraces the world all it's dimensions

Bengel had the following to say concerning: Gnomon = A **gnomon** (['noʊmɒn], from Greek γνώμων, *gnōmōn*, literally: "one that knows or examines") is the part of a sundial that casts the shadow.

Bengel's famous rule for determining a textual variant was "The more difficult reading is to be preferred", reasoning that it was more likely

---

[70] Arnold, Clinton E.; Exegetical Commentary On The New Testament: Ephesians. Grand Rapids, MI. Zondervan pg. 215,216.

that a scribe would change a more difficult reading to an easier one than vice versa.[71]

God's Word needs to be considered as something relatively simple, yet with inexhaustible riches. The closest associated subject to the dimensions of v18 is the love of Christ[72]. There are no ellipsis' present here that could be used to import a foreign idea into the topic manner.

All through this Great Prayer of Ephesians we see Paul working to instill in the reader a sense of the vast greatness and riches of the salvation that was won for them by what Jesus Christ accomplished on the cross. Paul is also trying to show them that the event of the crucifixion and the resurrection has changed history for the reader.

> Ephesians 3:18
> Expanded Translation
> [18] may be able as a direct result of the holy spirit that resides in you, be able to understand with all the saints what is the breadth which extends to all races and peoples and the length which spans from eternity to everlasting, and the depth that is so low no part of the creation can ascertain it, and the height that is far above all principalities (leading to the very right hand of God),

---

[71] Ibid

[72] Several textual variants exist that say instead of "the love of Christ" the text should read "the love of God" P46 uses "the exceeding knowledgeable love of Christ" Bruce Metzger reports that several witnesses P46, B 462 Coptics omit τε εἰζ and instead read πληρωθῇ πᾶν τὸ πλῆρωμα του θεου. "that all the fulness of God may be filled up"

Ephesians 3:19

This verse is a completion of verse 18[73]. It provides the subject of the four dimensions, still keeping the idea that the Love of Christ is beyond the ability of human knowledge to comprehend. Each verse is building upon the other. It is building up in what the believer has in Christ Jesus, basically informing the reader that what God has available for them exceeds all the wealth of the world.

> Ephesians 3:19
> KJV
> **[19]** And to know the love of Christ, which passeth knowledge, that ye might be filled with all the fulness of God.

> Ephesians 3:19
> RSV
> **[19]** and to know the love of Christ which surpasses knowledge, that you may be filled with all the fulness of God.

> Ephesians 3:19
> NIV
> **[19]** and to know this love that surpasses knowledge— that you may be filled to the measure of all the fullness of God.

---

[73] **** There are several textual variants found in several MSS exchanging the "Love of Christ" = "Love of God."

Ephesians 3:19
Aramaic Peshitta Version
[19] and would know the greatness of the knowledge of
the love of Meshikha and would be filled with all the
fullness of Alaha.

Ephesians 3:19
Darby
19 and to know the love of the Christ which surpasses
knowledge; that ye may be filled [even] to all the fulness
of God.

`Ephesians 3:19
Tyndale Ploughboy New Testament
[19] also to wite the charite of Crist more excellent than
science, that ye be fillid in al the plentee of God.

Paul's request for the believers in this verse demonstrates his passion
for the believers' understanding of the Love of Christ as spoken of
in v18. In Greek the words "to know" the love of Christ is the Greek
word γινώσκω. The word was used in Greek to denote the intelligent
comprehension of an object. It infers a practical and intelligent
understanding, and an experiential understanding. This understanding
was not just a partial understanding. The carpenters and tradesmen not
only understood the work that they needed to perform but also, they
had completed projects previously and had the intimate knowledge of
the tools, techniques, mediums in which they worked.

II Timothy 2:15
RSV
[**15**] Do your best to present yourself to God as one
approved, a **workman** who has no need to be ashamed,
rightly handling the word of truth.

Kittel's says that the execution of γινώσκειν is not primarily related to
one particular organ or limited to one particular mode. It relates to the

knowledge acquired through experiences both good and bad.[74] Homer uses the word as a familiarity between two people.

> Homer Odyssey 15, 537
> [535] Then wise Telemachus answered him again: "Ah, stranger, I would that [γινώσκειν] of kindness and many a gift from me, so that one that met thee would call thee blessed."

γινώσκειν is a knowledge of what is a reality. This knowledge is certified and verified. The Greeks believed that eye is a more reliable witness and to be more trusted than the ear. Culturally the Greeks looked down upon the blind citizens as being unreliable in any discussion as what they said could not be "verified"

Heraclitus of Ephesus alluded to the lack of understanding in Fragment #5

> Heraclitus FR 5
> The majority of people have no understanding of the things with which they daily meet, nor, when instructed, do they have any right knowledge of them, although to themselves they seem to have.

Verification was primarily through sight and observation. Complete knowledge comes as a byproduct of sight. Knowledge was regarded as a mode of sight. In the Greek world the question of truth implies that of the reality underlying all appearances as true reality. The understanding of knowledge as that which compromises this truth is shaped accordingly.[75]

γινώσκω is at the very foundation of what the Greeks held as an understanding of heart, or the seat of all knowledge within them.

---

[74] Kittel, Gerhard: Theological Dictionary Of The New Testament. Grand Rapids, MI. Wm. B. Eerdmans Publishing Company. 1964, Vol 1 pg. 689
[75] Ibid pg. 692

The acquisition of knowledge was a never-ending lifelong pursuit. The enlightenment of the soul was to be found in the complete understanding of one's carnal knowledge. Knowledge has at its center the characteristic of seeing and discernment of the truth of what was seen. Emotionally, knowledge and the pursuit of it bring with them the emotions of fear and courage, sadness and happiness. Emotions worked in the processing of knowledge and the verification of it.

Hellenism and Gnostics is to some extent prepared by classical development[76] The Mystery religions of the day would disperse secret knowledge to its adherents in their quest for salvation. The following of the cultic religions has its own γινώσκω, which was passed to their adherents for guidance, salvation, and the search for self. γνῶσις connotes not only knowing but also the pursuance of knowledge and wisdom[77].

> Proverbs 1:2-7
> KJV
> [2] To know wisdom and instruction; to perceive the words of understanding;
> [3] To receive the instruction of wisdom, justice, and judgment, and equity;
> [4] To give subtlety to the simple, to the young man knowledge and
> [5] A wise man will hear, and will increase learning; and a man of understanding shall attain unto wise counsels:
> [6] To understand a proverb, and the interpretation; the words of the wise, and their dark sayings.
> [7] The fear of the LORD is the beginning of knowledge: but fools despise wisdom and instruction.

---

[76] Ibid

[77] Consider Knowledge as the information desired while wisdom is the practical application of the knowledge. Both together is the end result of γνῶσις

Volumes have been written by philosophers and theologians trying to define both knowledge and wisdom. The first use of knowledge was in the Garden of Eden.

> Genesis 2:9
> KJV
> [9] And out of the ground made the LORD God to grow every tree that is pleasant to the sight, and good for food; the tree of life also in the midst of the garden, and the tree of **knowledge** of good and evil.

Though it appears as such, the knowledge of good and evil was not and is not a black and white, yes or no proposition. As we see today, there are many factors that determine right from wrong. To properly render a verdict, knowledge itself without prejudice is the chief factor required. We need to see that Paul's petition to God here is, so we may know by experience.

> Exodus 33:3
> KJV
> [3] And I have filled him with the spirit of God, in wisdom, and in understanding, and in knowledge, and in all manner of workmanship,

Understanding (σύνεσις) is considered to be the bridge between wisdom and knowledge. σύνεσις is thought to be the point in the brain where all knowledge flows together to bring a complete knowledge to the man. The end result of knowledge and wisdom should be σύνεσις. This to the Greeks was the complete goal of the acquiring of γινώσκω.

The love of Christ is the focus of the knowledge discussed in this verse. Some texts say the "love of God" however the oldest known MSS uses the "love of Christ[78]".

---

[78] p.45, p46 and p91

Love is expressed by three different Greek words, φιλω. αγαπεο, and ερός. φιλω is also known as a brotherly love. It is the love that is available to the man of body and soul. This can be a very strong form of love as man and wife, mother and child etc. It differs from αγαπεο in that it does not take its root in God's love. ερός is a sexual form of "love". It is totally physical in nature. In English it is the act of making love, sexual activity. In the cultic religions it is a rite of worship. Corinth was a seat of pagan religion with its several hundred temple prostitutes. They were there to help the worshippers fulfill their religious duties. Pompeii was very involved with a sexual form of love, ερός. The cost of the prostitutes was actually less than the cost of a loaf of bread in the marketplace[79].

To the Greeks, γινώσκειν is the cultivated methodical activity of the active νοῦς or λόγος, fulfilled in science and mathematics and particularly philosophy. The γνῶσις of the Gnostics is bot the process and the result. The Gnostics believed that γνῶσις is a χάρισμα (gift) which is from God[80].

> Proverbs 1:7
> KJV
> [7] The fear of the LORD is the beginning of knowledge:
> but fools despise wisdom and instruction.

The Gnostics also considered γνῶσις as an ecstatic and mystical vision. To this idea knowing is still understood as a kind of seeing. Once again sight is the most important organ where knowledge is understood.

The best way to picture γνῶσις is as a point where all the rivers of knowledge come together. In this junction all the rivers add to the process of understanding. Looked at from the Word's perspective, sight is not the principal organ in understanding.

---

[79] Approx. $1.35 in today's currency (2019).
[80] Kittel, Gerhard: Theological Dictionary Of The New Testament. Grand Rapids, MI. Wm. B. Eerdmans Publishing Company. 1964, Vol 1 pg. 694

Romans 10:14-18

KJV

[14] How then shall they call on him in whom they have not believed? and how shall they believe in him of whom they have not heard? and how shall they hear without a preacher?

[15] And how shall they preach, except they be sent? as it is written, How beautiful are the feet of them that preach the gospel of peace, and bring glad tidings of good things!

[16] But they have not all obeyed the gospel. For Esaias saith, Lord, who hath believed our report?

[17] So then faith cometh by hearing, and hearing by the word of God.

[18] But I say, Have they not heard? Yes verily, their sound went into all the earth, and their words unto the ends of the world.

It is the hearing of the Word of God and not sight that brings a man to repentance. As time goes on there is continually more understanding developed.

The Shepherd of Hermes had an interesting concept of Mind saying the mind is of God's very essence "The mind is not separated of God's essentiality, but is united onto it as light onto the sun. This Mind in men is God and for this cause some of mankind are gods and their humanity is nigh unto divinity. For good Daimon said gods are immortal men and men are mortal gods.[81]

Of course, this brings in the great lie that Satan introduced to Eve:

Genesis 3:1-6

RSV

Now the serpent was more subtle than any other wild creature that the LORD God had made. He said to the

---

[81] Shepherd of Hermes - Corp Herm, XIII

woman, "Did God say, `You shall not eat of any tree of the garden'?"

[2] And the woman said to the serpent, "We may eat of the fruit of the trees of the garden;

[3] but God said, `You shall not eat of the fruit of the tree which is in the midst of the garden, neither shall you touch it, lest you die.'"

[4] But the serpent said to the woman, "You will not die.

[5] For God knows that when you eat of it your eyes will be opened, and you will be like God, knowing good and evil."

The great lie was two parts, first, you shall not surely die, which then says that man reaches immortality. When he dies, he immediately goes to heaven, which voids the reason for Christ to return if true. Number two is the idea that man could be a god, with all the power, recognition, authority and of course, praise, which was intended to be only for God, that comes with that. Remember that Julius Caesar was deified after his death. Knowledge does not bring other of these things to pass.

The ἀγάπην του χριστοῦ (Love of Christ) is the proper wording here. It is very simple to realize that the fullness of the Godhead dwells in our Lord. Jesus Christ acts as the agent between God and mortal men. There are a few MSS that present the idea of [82] ἀγάπην του θεοῦ. Most of these are obscure fragments of MSS, especially in the Coptic, and Ethiopic texts. "The love of Christ" is the correct translation.[83] Bruce Metzger makes no mention of the textual variants.

> I Thessalonians 5:16-18
> NIV
> [16] Rejoice always,
> [17] Pray Continually
> [18] Give thanks in all circumstances; for this is God's will for you in Christ Jesus

---

[82] Please see Appendix C - P46 translation

[83] Bruce Metzger makes no mention of the textual variants

I Thessalonians 5:16-18
KJV
[16] Rejoice evermore.
[17] Pray without ceasing.
[18] In everything give thanks: for this is the will of
God in Christ Jesus concerning you.

This verse shows that God was in Christ and the will of God concerning us is expressed here "Rejoice evermore" and "Pray without ceasing".

Colossians 1:27
KJV
[27] To whom God would make known what is the
riches of the glory of this mystery among the Gentiles;
which is **Christ in you**, the hope of glory:

This verse draws everything together as God in Christ and Christ is in you. This gives authority and verification to the believer.

Mark 16:17
KJV
[17] And these signs shall follow them that believe; In
my name shall they cast out devils; they shall speak with
new tongues;

Mark 16:17
NIV
[17] And these signs will accompany those who believe:
In my name they will drive out demons; they will speak
in new tongues;

Though in this verse they did not have the spirit of God present in them, the spirit at this time was upon them. Now with Christ in us all believers have the authority and the ability to perform miracles and bring out signs and wonders. Martin Luther had stated that to understand the Love of Christ was greater than the understanding of all other knowledge.

The verse begins with ινῶναι τε τήν ὑπερβαλλονσαν τῆς γνωσεως αγάπην τοῦ χριστοῦ. – "And to know the knowledge surpassing the love of Christ". νῶςαι is not in any way dependent upon Καταλαβε σθαι but stands on its own and also in unison with it.[84] The participle τε does not become a branch but rather it adds a clause that is not dependent upon the previous clause.

This clause puts this verse in harmony with the previous prayer of Ephesians as shown in the following verses:

> Ephesians 1:16-20
> KJV
> [16] Cease not to give thanks for you, making mention of you in my prayers;
> [17] That the God of our Lord Jesus Christ, the Father of glory, may give unto you the spirit of wisdom and revelation in the knowledge of him:
> [18] The eyes of your understanding being enlightened; that ye may know what is the hope of his calling, and what the riches of the glory of his inheritance in the saints,
> [19] And what is the exceeding greatness of his power to usward who believe, according to the working of his mighty power,
> [20] Which he wrought in Christ, when he raised him from the dead, and set him at his own right hand in the heavenly places,

This verse has seen several theologians attempt to place the translation of this verse in such a way that it establishes their own theological viewpoint. For example Conibears inserts an unwarranted phrase here

---

[84] Moulton, Harold K. The Analytical Greek Lexicon revised 1978 Edition, Grand Rapids, MI. The Zondervan Corporation pg. 542.

that reads "filleth therewith with Christ's love even to the measure of the fulness of God."[85].

One must not and cannot take the subject of sin too lightly. In both prayers God provides for Christendom an advocate for sin. In Ephesians 1:20 God provides Jesus Christ to be the advocate for sin. In the prayer of Chapter 3, God provides the holy spirit to be the other advocate for sin before Him (See Ephesians 3:16).

The proposition εἰς is used here with special caution. The simple dative could have been used here however εἰς does not stand for ἐν. it does not connote "with" but rather "Into" or "For". Eadie renders the it as "filled up to" or "unto", an end quantitative considered. The whole fulness of God can never contract itself so as to lodge in any one created heart, but the smaller vessel may have its own fulness poured into it from one of the larger dimensions.[86]. The fulness of God in all its communicable glory will in every element of it impact itself capaciously into the exalted bosom, for Christ dwells in their hearts. This makes the difference between God and his adopted sons (called saints) to not be in kind as this would lose the freewill of the individual. Rather, the difference will lie in degree and extent. The believer always has the option to either walk according the world, without God and without hope, or to walk on the path God sets before him. Usually these changes in the text come as a result of an adherence to particular denominational traditions, or as the writer's viewpoint and attempt to reason something to their own belief system. The danger of this idea is that the scriptures are to be of no private interpretation. But the attempt is clear as they try to make what is said to fall into their own belief system. i.e. If they cannot believe that Jesus fed the 5,000 with six fishes and several loads of bread, many will bring more vendors in till they had enough to fill everyone.

In the East when a man was married, at some point soon after the wedding he would take leave of his wife.

---

[85] Eadie, John., Commentary On The Epistle To The Ephesians, Minneapolis, Minnesota. James and Klock Christian Publishing Co, pg. 259
[86] Ibid

FRANK ABISSI JR. TH.D., PH.D.

John 14:1-4

KJV

[1] Let not your heart be troubled: ye believe in God, believe also in me.

[2] In my Father's house are many mansions: if it were not so, I would have told you. I go to prepare a place for you.

[3] And if I go and prepare a place for you, I will come again, and receive you unto myself; that where I am, there ye may be also.

[4] And whither I go ye know, and the way ye know.

Jesus was speaking here as a husband would speak to his wife - Let not your heart be troubled, ye believe in God, believe also in me. Here he is promising that he would protect his spouse from whatever fear she has. Next, "In my father's house there are many apartments", he is talking about her basic needs of shelter, food. During this time period he is away from her, he is getting set to provide for her. This is a demonstrated manner of the love of Christ, like a bridegroom and the Bride (Israel).

Romans 8 also talks about the love of Christ. Here, Paul is discussing the role of the bridegroom with the Bride in the Grace dispensation.

Romans 8:35

KJV

[35] Who shall separate us from the **love of Christ**? shall tribulation, or distress, or persecution, or famine, or nakedness, or peril, or sword?

Once again here we see in the same vein of John 14 that the bridegroom vows to protect the bride. The analogy set here of the love of Christ is of the role of the bridegroom and bride, and the love expressed between the two. The boundaries of love are seen here, as nothing will separate the believer from the love of Christ. Ephesians shows the enormity of the love with measurements or dimensions. Understanding that the

Love of Christ has at its very core the love of God. This love becomes an absolute limitless resource.

II Corinthians 5:14 shows the second of the three usages of the "love of Christ" in the Grace Administration.

> II Corinthians 5:13-17
> KJV
> [13] For whether we be beside ourselves, it is to God: or whether we be sober, it is for your cause.
> [14] For the love of Christ constraineth us; because we thus judge, that if one died for all, then were all dead:
> [15] And that he died for all, that they which live should not henceforth live unto themselves, but unto him which died for them, and rose again.
> [16] Wherefore henceforth know we no man after the flesh: yea, though we have known Christ after the flesh, yet now henceforth know we him no more.
> [17] Therefore if any man be in Christ, he is a new creature: old things are passed away; behold, all things are become new.

To constrain means in a general sense, to strain; to press; to urge; to drive; to exert force, physical or moral, either in urging to action or in restraining it. Similar to peer pressure in its effect, it compels or forces one to a work of some type. It is to urge with an irresistible power or a strength sufficient to produce a desired effect. This is a factor in determining the strength that the love of Christ has on an individual. The constraining is to move a person to perform "good works". In religious service[87] there are only a few different things that can be done, prayer, praise, giving of thanks and good works. There are very few actions outside of these that can be done that would fulfill the requirements of religious service[88].

---

[87] Romans 12:1
[88] See Isaiah 58 for the true fast.

FRANK ABISSI JR. TH.D., PH.D.

In this section Paul is identifying the strength that the believers must possess to grasp the knowledge of the Love of Christ. The NIV translates these verses very remarkably.

Ephesians 3:18,19
NIV
[18] may have power, together with all the Lord's holy people, to grasp how wide and long and high and deep is the love of Christ,
[19] and to know this love that surpasses knowledge—that you may be filled to the measure of all the fullness of God.

"To know this love that surpasses" is a clause where the limits of logic are strained. We could sense that Paul is taxing his lexicon, we see Paul is finding the words which are at the limits of vocabulary in his explanation of the love of Christ. Snodgrass[89] states "this is the language from someone who has been surprised and overwhelmed with Christ's love" and a surface description of it. Words cannot and never will be able to fully describe the true depth, breadth and height of this love.

Paradoxically, to understand and to grasp the love of Christ is beyond any human comprehension. Paul, though, is petitioning God to give them an advanced understanding of that love. For believers the vastness of the love can never be exhausted. The Love of Christ itself becomes the foundation in which the believer becomes rooted and founded. Yet this love is not a static spiritual love. The idea is that the believer can grow within this love to share with others. The Christian is to build upon the relationship with Jesus Christ and then use that relationship of love and share it with others.

---

[89] Klyne Ryland Snodgrass is an American Theologian who served as a professor at the North Park Seminary in Chicago His book : Stories with intent : a Comprehensive guide to the Parables of Jesus is without rival in its field

In this verse Paul starts with the word τὲ, which could be translated "indeed" which is an emphatic usage of the word. The only translation that brings this to the forefront is the Aramaic Peshitta version:

Ephesians 3:19
Aramaic Peshitta Version
[19] and would know the greatness of the knowledge of the love of Meshikha and would be filled with all the fullness of Alaha.

This emphatic is all but ignored in the other texts, yet its purpose is to bring an emphasis to the acquiring the knowledge of the love of Christ. The Aramaic translates the word as "greatness" which is a very good translation.

This verse introduces the second intercessory petition with the use of the word ἱνα, and the third time it is used in the prayer it is rendered "in order that". Referring back to the chart "Ephesians 3:14-21 Introversion and Alternation" this is attached to the second intercessory petition as a final petition. So, Paul's prayer is that "they may be filled with all the fulness of God". There are two other times that the words "fulness of God" or "fulness of Christ is used".

Ephesians 4:13
RSV
[13] until we all attain to the unity of the faith and of the knowledge of the Son of God, to mature manhood, to the measure of the stature of the fulness of Christ;

This verse is in the practical treatise of Ephesians and coincides with the practical treatise of Ephesians dealing with the Body fitly joined, which is directly parallel to the Temple fitly framed.

Doctrinal and Practical Treatises concerning
The Temple and the Body

G| The Temple fitly framed 2:19-22
H| The Mystery 3:1-13
I| Prayer 3:14-21
H| The One Body 4:1-6
G| The Body fitly joined 4:7-16

The third usage of these words is found in Colossians 1:19

Colossians 1:15-19
RSV
[15] He is the image of the invisible God, the first-born of all creation;
[16] for in him all things were created, in heaven and on earth, visible and invisible, whether thrones or dominions or principalities or authorities -- all things were created through him and for him.
[17] He is before all things, and in him all things hold together.
[18] He is the head of the body, the church; he is the beginning, the first-born from the dead, that in everything he might be pre-eminent.
[19] For in him all the fulness of God was pleased to dwell,

The three uses of these words bring in the believer being filled with all the fulness of Christ. The second (Ephesians 4:13) brings in the idea that the measure of the stature of the fulness of Christ is available to every believer. In the third we see that since the believer has Christ indwelling in him so then the fulness of God is pleased to dwell in the Christian.

Bullinger points to an Ellipsis in this verse that cannot be ignored. The figure of speech is an Ellipsis (Absolute: of the pronoun) He mentions that the verse should read thus:

> Ephesians 3:18
> KJV
> [18] That ye being rooted and grounded in love may know what is the breadth [*of it*] and length [*of it*] and the depth [*of it*] and the height [*of it*] *i.e.* of love.[90]

The word "filled" πλήρης used here denotes a state of complete fullness. Used in a nautical sense, it is a ship that is fully manned, fully rigged with new lines, absolutely ready for its voyage. In relation to time, it is the overflow of the eternally flowing streams.[91] It is the satisfied fulness of the soul. In the LXX we find it used of a vessel (cistern) flowing abundantly and overflowing.

> I Kings 17:14,16
> KJV
> [14] For thus saith the LORD God of Israel, The barrel of meal shall not waste, neither shall the **cruse of** oil fail, until the day that the LORD sendeth rain upon the earth.
> [16] And the barrel of meal wasted not, neither did the **cruse of** oil fail, according to the word of the LORD, which he spake by Elijah.

From a Christian perspective, it marks that not only is the Christian filled with the love of Christ, he or she is also overflowing with it. The human vessel we have is too restricted to contain it all. πλήρης to be in this state is to be a fully equipped believer in the Lord. Because of this the ability to put on the full armor of God becomes available:

---

[90] Bullinger, E.W.; Figures of Speech Used In The Bible, Ann Arbor Michigan, Baker Book House Company pg. 18

[91] Kittel, Gerhard: Theological Dictionary Of The New Testament. Grand Rapids, MI. Wm. B. Eerdmans Publishing Company. Vol 4, Pg. 283

Ephesians 6:10-18
KJV
[10] Finally, my brethren, be strong in the Lord, and in the power of his might.
[11] Put on the whole armor of God, that ye may be able to stand against the wiles of the devil.
[12] For we wrestle not against flesh and blood, but against principalities, against powers, against the rulers of the darkness of this world, against spiritual wickedness in high places.
[13] Wherefore take unto you the whole armor of God, that ye may be able to withstand in the evil day, and having done all, to stand.
[14] Stand therefore, having your loins girt about with truth, and having on the breastplate of righteousness;
[15] And your feet shod with the preparation of the gospel of peace;
[16] Above all, taking the shield of faith, wherewith ye shall be able to quench all the fiery darts of the wicked.
[17] And take the helmet of salvation, and the sword of the Spirit, which is the word of God:
[18] Praying always with all prayer and supplication in the Spirit, and watching thereunto with all perseverance and supplication for all saints;

The entire fabric of Ephesians fits completely together. The disregard of any one section means that entire epistle would fall apart. You cannot have any of the doctrinal or practical treatises removed if the Epistle is relied upon to stand on its own.

Ephesians 3:19
Expanded Translation
And to experience the tranquility of the love of Christ which is far beyond knowledge, that your life will become one of being filled and overflowing with the fulness of our Father's love.

Ephesians 3:20

The next two verses, a doxology, are typical of all Jewish writings. Prayers were ended with a blessing to God, so oftentimes the payer ended with "forever and ever".

> I Chronicles 16:36
> Darby
> **[36]** Blessed be Jehovah the God of Israel, from eternity and to eternity! And all the people said, Amen! and praised Jehovah.

> I Chronicles 16:36
> KJV
> [**36**] Blessed be the LORD God of Israel for ever and ever. And all the people said, Amen, and praised the LORD.

The conclusion of the verse according to the Puritan Exposition of Ephesians, is as follows in praise and thanksgiving:

Ephesians 3:20,21 Conclusions:92

1. The Person Praised is Set Down.
2. The Persons Praising
3. The Mediator
4. The Durance[93]

---

[92] Goodwin, Thomas and Bayne, Paul., Puritan Exposition Of Ephesians. Sovereign Grace Book Club 1958 Book II pg. 206
[93] Durance is middle English for endurance or the passing of time

The Jews also customarily responded to prayers made by the Pharisees or any other Elder of the church who was praying with a benediction of "Amen[94]" or translated "so be it".

Ephesians 3:20
KJV
[20] Now unto him that is able to do exceeding abundantly above all that we ask or think, according to the power that worketh in us,

Ephesians 3:20
RSV
[20] Now to him who by the power at work within us is able to do far more abundantly than all that we ask or think,

Ephesians 3:20
Aramaic Peshitta
[20] Now to him who is able, by surpassing power, to do even more for us than what we ask and think, according to his power that is performed in us

Ephesians 3:20
NIV
[20] Now to him who is able to do immeasurably more than all we ask or imagine, according to his power that is at work within us,

Ephesians 3:20
Darby
[20] But to him that is able to do far exceedingly above all which we ask or think, according to the power which works in us,

---

[94] The letter A is long in verbal prayers, it is sung with a short A at the end of a song.

Ephesians 3:20
Tyndales Ploughboy Edition
[20] Vnto him that is able to do excedynge aboudantly above all that we axe or thynke accordynge to the power that worketh in vs.

The beginning of Paul's conclusion of the prayer is extremely strong in its vocabulary. If could be considered that this is the end of his prayer, as the use of the conjunction δε clearly signals a break from what is proceeding. Paul also assures the believers that God is ready to commit to the performance or what He has promised. The promises that are written before could be considered too expansive in their magnitude, but here Paul is assuring the Ephesians that the promises are not too expansive and yes, God is ready to perform. In no uncertain terms God can do all that He promises, and absolutely nothing hinders God's ability. The powerful language that Paul brings into the end of the prayer to "Him who is able", gives validation to the prayer. "Unto him" has to refer to God alone, no other possesses the ability to do exceeding abundantly above all that we ask or think, and no other is deserving to receive glory in the church throughout all ages. In these verses the pronoun "him" is used in place of the name "God". There is not a figure of speech present here, though "him" is definitely the focus of the doxology here in these verses.

God can perform the unimaginable in His people because of His invincible potency and His indwelling experience. Here Paul is directing his speech to the one who is able to do exceedingly abundantly above all that can be asked or thought. Consider this in light of verse 18, an attempt to bring a concept of the greatness of God is brought here, while in verse 20 we see that God is able to do even greater than these things. Paul was accustomed to asking God for extravagant things on behalf of all and any of the believers. This doxology fits perfectly here because Paul's previous intercessory petition of verse 18. This doxology fits with the first element of the other New Testament prayers and other doxologies in the naming or mention of to whom it is addressed. Paul's language and vocabulary seem to be stretched to its limit in this verse.

He finds it necessary to use a rare compound adverb, "ὑπερεκπερισσοῦ" which could be properly translated into English as "infinitely more than". He is trying to bring across to the believers the idea that there is no limit and nothing that God cannot do for them. This exalted doxology of course signals a break from the intercessory petitions and it also gives the assurance to the believers that God can fulfill the prayer and all His resources are available to them. Paul is basically affirming that if there were any question as to whether God could fulfill the requests of the heart, the answer would be a resounding yes.

The last phrase can be translated two ways. ἐν ἡμῖν can be translated as either "within us" or "amongst us". Either translation can be considered correct because Jesus taught:

> Matthew 18:19
> KJV
> [19] Again I say unto you, That if **two** of you shall agree
> on earth as touching anything that they shall ask, it
> shall be done for them of my Father which is in heaven.

The beginning of the next verse starts with the defining of the potential power "Now unto him that is able to do..." this brings in two elements to consider, the first being time. This marks the time of the prayer, which makes it an immediate consequential petitionary phrase. The prayer as spoken in verse 18, length makes it timeless. The urgency of the prayer is now, yet for every Christian it is an immediate prayer.

God always prefers that the prayers of His children come from their hearts. He has never been one to worry concerning syntax. For example, the "Lord's Prayer"

> Matthew 6:1-9
> KJV
> [1] Take heed that ye do not your alms before men, to
> be seen of them: otherwise ye have no reward of your
> Father which is in heaven.

[2] Therefore when thou doest thine alms, do not sound a trumpet before thee, as the hypocrites do in the synagogues and in the streets, that they may have glory of men. Verily I say unto you, They have their reward.

[3] But when thou doest alms, let not thy left hand know what thy right hand doeth:

[4] That thine alms may be in secret: and thy Father which seeth in secret himself shall reward thee openly.

[5] And when thou prayest, thou shalt not be as the hypocrites are: for they may be seen of men. Verily I say unto you, They have their

[6] But thou, when thou prayest, enter into thy closet, and when thou hast shut thy door, pray to thy Father which is in secret; and thy Father which seeth in secret shall reward thee openly.

[7] But when ye pray, use not vain repetitions, as the heathen do: for they think that they shall be heard for their much speaking.

[8] Be not ye therefore like unto them: for your Father knoweth what things ye have need of, before ye ask him.

[9] After this manner therefore pray ye: Our Father which art in heaven, Hallowed be thy name.

The Lord's Prayer has a distinction of being an instruction in prayer. Matthew 6:1-9 renders instructions on how to pray. This is much like the prayer of Ephesians being a great example of how to pray as an individual in the household of God. The prayers in Romans stand as an example of being a believer and his relationship to God. The Great Prayer of Ephesians stands as an example of how-to prayer corporately as a member of the family of God. Each and every member has the right, privilege and opportunity to pray within and for the Church of God.

From the context we can see that this prayer is addressed to God our Father. The previous noun is in verse 19, "that ye may be filled with all the fulness of God". The entire great prayer directs its petitions to

God, the Father of our of Jesus Christ. P46 points to God the Father
in its reading:

Ephesians 3:20
p46[95]
now to one empowered beyond all things to do over
abundantly we inquire or we think according to power
operating in us

For each verse in the Bible is it important that we determine to whom
it is addressed. For instance, in Old Testament of greatest import was
that the Mosaic law was completely fulfilled. The law was considered
nullified with what Jesus Christ accomplished for us on the cross.
Salvation before the day of the birth of the church was determined to be
by the adherence to the Mosaic law. After the day of Pentecost a believer
had to adhere to Romans 10:9,10. The verses that made up the Mosaic
law were now null and void; the new law of love was the order. The
Greek uses the word δυναμένῳ the phrase: "to him who is able to do."
δυναμαι is defined as "to be able" and "to be capable of", from which
we find our English word "dynamite". δυναμαι shows a measure of
potential power. To be able and actually doing are two different things.
All words derived from the root δυνα, have their basic meaning of being
able to, to have the strength in reserve, to have a capability, which is a
virtue of ability. δυνα stresses the factuality of the ability. The stress
falls upon being able[96]. The believer has been imbued with the power of
God and can call upon it whenever the need arises. However, it is not
until the power comes into usage that the power becomes an ενεργεμα
or power put into operation. The holy spirit within each Christian
supplies the necessary power to live a life of abundance. The noun
form of the word δυνατος means one who has the capability, power, or
ability. It usually is used as "one who has the power". It seems the nature
of origin of the power has been expressed in myriad of different ways.
Plato had a different perspective.

---

[95] See Appendix 3 - p46

[96] Kittel, Gerhard: Theological Dictionary Of The New Testament. Grand
Rapids, MI. Wm. B. Eerdmans Publishing Company. Vol II pg. 284

Plato Resp. v., 477cd
Shall awe say that the powers belong to that kind go existing things by which we... can do was we can do... In a faculty (power) I cannot see color or any shape or similar mark such as those which in many cases I can fix my eyes to discriminate in my thought one thing of another. But in the case of a faculty I look to that only - that to which it is related and what it effects, and it is this way that I come to call each one of them a faculty and that which is related to the same thing and accomplishes the same thing, I call the same faculty, and that to another I call.

It is of great interest to note that in verses 20 and 21, Bullinger does not list any figures of speech. However, there is a very prime example of Epizeuxis present here[97] "unto him that is" and "unto him be". The words "unto him that is able to do...." "is an identifier - dynamic, while "unto him be glory in the church" is an identifier, passive.

When looking at the group of words which make their root in δυνα, we find that δύναμις is by far the most important word in the group. It has a singular, substantive construction to it. The original meaning of ability or capability is very well preserved. Aristotle preserves the meaning very well, however he debates whether the power is an immediate form or developmental [i.e., is God developmental or does he have all the strength he has always had.[98]] This could be debated all day by the philosophers, however the Bible says that the power of God is a constant and not a developmental power,

Hebrews 13:6-8
KJV
[6] Hence we can confidently say, "The Lord is my helper,
I will not be afraid; what can man do to me?"

---

[97] Epizeuxis or Duplication is the replication of the same word in the same sense.
[98] Aristotle Metaph. VIII, 8, Pg. 1049b 24

[7] Remember your leaders, those who spoke to you the word of God; consider the outcome of their life, and imitate their faith.

[8] Jesus Christ is the same yesterday and today and forever.

So the δύναμις talked about here is at its full strength from the time the person becomes a Christian and then throughout eternity. The question then arises "why doesn't man utilizes this great strength?"

I Corinthians 12:4-11
RSV
[4]Now there are varieties of gifts, but the same Spirit;
[5] and there are varieties of service, but the same Lord;
[6] and there are varieties of working, but it is the same God who inspires them all in every one.
[7] To each is given the manifestation of the Spirit for the common good.
[8] To one is given through the Spirit the utterance of wisdom, and to another the utterance of knowledge according to the same Spirit,
[9] to another faith by the same Spirit, to another gifts of healing by the one Spirit,
[10] to another the working of miracles, to another prophecy, to another the ability to distinguish between spirits, to another various kinds of tongues, to another the interpretation of tongues.
[11] All these are inspired by one and the same Spirit, who apportions to each one individually as he wills.

Quite simply, man does not choose to operate the powers that God has given to him. From this verse we find that the problem with these "gifts" is not the ability of their working but rather the usage of them "All these are inspired by one and the same Spirit," Many simply do not believe they exist or they believe several but not all exist "who apportions to each one individually as he wills." One of the sources of these problems is the fact that these are thought to be gifts in themselves.

> I Corinthians 12:7
> RSV
> [12] Who apportions to each one individually as he wills.

The so-called gifts are not nine separate gifts at all but rather they are manifestations or separate operations of the one gift of holy spirit.

Ephesians 3:20,21 work together as a clear doxology, showing to the readers what the greatness of God is, what the response they should have concerning what was written all throughout the seven doctrinal treatises and what the first two intercessory petitions should provide. The beginning of the 3:20 "Now unto him who is able to do" is a very familiar word in this section - "δύναμαι the power that God is able to demonstrate for his people. So, this is saying that God is the one who has the power to do what follows. In essence it is providing a CV of God's credentials to do exceedingly abundantly above all that we ask or think.

"Exceedingly abundantly above" is just one simple word ηυπερ. In the accusative it is simply "over and above, in behalf of". Thus far in this verse we have a potential for great power that is over and above, on behalf of. The verse could be looked at as being a power over and above what is and has been known to man all on behalf of the son, "Jesus Christ." To "ask" is very simply an inquiry. When we look at the word for mind: voέω we see that this is not just a passive thought. It means to direct one's mind to a subject, to actively notice and perceive, in the sense of receiving both mental and sensual perception. This is more than just an inattentive impression in the mind, this is an indelible impression that is coming to the mind through at least two of the five senses. It is meaning to think and understand, as it becomes part of the mind of the man. voέω is not just the organ of the mind, but rather it is the sum of the whole of the thoughts that bring knowledge to the man. These are the thoughts that stay with and become a part of the person. So, we have here a power that is over and above all others, and the power has its genesis in the mind that is a very part of the person. God is able to be all for all in all.

Still, this part of the mind is not required to have spirit to understand it. It can be understood by the single verse:

> Romans 1:20
> KJV
> [20] For the invisible things of him from the creation
> of the world are clearly seen, being understood (νοέω)
> by the things that are made, even his eternal power and
> Godhead; so that they are without excuse:

This knowledge is not a part of the ancient cultic religions, it is clearly understandable by all, yet once achieved, it becomes a part of the person's thought processes. Philo of Alexandria used it of Adam hiding himself in the Garden from the Lord[99]. We also see that Philo compared Noah with Moses. Philo shows that in the lives of both of these men they were studying the synthetic locution "to find grace"[100]. Then he provides a series of three possible interpretations, three hypotheses which progress gradually in depth of meaning. He states that if Noah had the good will of the Powers, instead of considering there to be a small contradiction, the reader of Philo would find a similarity here. The first of the three hypotheses here mark out a moral itinerary instead of proposing an exclusive and logical theory in this comparison.[101] Philo's examination of the Pentateuch seemed to dwell upon straight comparisons and the thoughts of the men in that time period. Philo, in his Ebr, stated that the two opposites together form a single whole by the division in which the opposites are known[102]. Since man was ousted from the Garden of Eden, he has endeavored to find two things. #1 that he should never die

---

[99] Philo Leg 1:3
[100] Philo Deus 109
[101] Ibid pg. 159
[102] Philo Ebr. 186

and have eternal life on his terms and #2 Man should be as God, with all the power that accompanies that desire. At the root of it all is pride, that man can do it himself without the help of God, that man could live with self-help, without the need for help from God. History has it that whenever man tried to take over and play the role of God, man failed. Whenever man came before God in all humility, man prospered. As man's Patron, God saw to it that man prospered. As the Patron, God supplied all the needs of man, and man lived in harmony with God.

There is a third aspect of God's power that must be discussed, and that is ενεργεο. This power is found in a sense of activity or performance of energy. The source of the energy is not always identified, but in the context, it is usually divine or demonic power. According to Kittel this word occurs one time in Wisdom, and II Maccabees and III Maccabees, thus there is no Hebrew original of this word[103] The word ενεργεο is widely used in connection with cosmic energy and power. When used in conjunction with δύναμις it signifies a cosmic phenomenon of very great proportions. The cosmic power awakens epic proportion of terror. This kind of strength is often considered to be κοσμοκράτορες.[104]

> Ephesians 6:12
> KJV
> [12] For we wrestle not against flesh and blood, but against principalities, against powers, against the rulers (κοσμοκράτορες) of the darkness of this world, against spiritual wickedness in high places.

> Ephesians 6:12
> NIV
> [12]For our struggle is not against flesh and blood, but against the rulers, against the authorities, against the powers of this dark world and against the spiritual forces of evil in the heavenly realms.

---

[103] Kittel, Gerhard: Theological Dictionary Of The New Testament. Grand Rapids, MI. Wm. B. Eerdmans Publishing Company. Vol II pg.652
[104] Ibid

The conclusion of this prayer is a beautiful doxology, bringing great praise to God. It does bring in the fact that God has this limitless power. This power is a prominent theme in all of the doxologies that Paul writes. This said, there is a special attribute to this Doxology in that it brings three types of God's power together: δύναμαι (verb), δύναμις, (noun) and ἐνεργέω. This verse, with the blending together of the three types of power is probably the strongest single doxology in the entire Word of God. It combines all this power, which is considered to be strong in a cosmos sense, a world sense and a spiritual sense. To bring a greater awareness of God's power to the readers Paul uses the statement "above all that we ask of think." God can do exceeding above -this puts a rhetorical stress on God's power to intervene and act on behalf of His people. This receives yet further emphasis by Paul's use of the adverb ὑπερεκπερισσοῦ.[105] The reader should understand that God has already proven His superior ability in each of these realms.

"Able to do exceedingly abundantly above all that we ask or think" requires the "we" be able to comprehend with all saints what is the breadth, length, depth and height. Without that degree of comprehension the ability of thought on that great of a scale is not possible.

> Isaiah 14:12-19
> NIV
> [12] How you have fallen from heaven, morning star, son of the dawn! You have been cast down to the earth, you who once laid low the nations!
> [13] You said in your heart, "I will ascend to the heavens; I will raise my throne above the stars of God I will sit enthroned on the mount of assembly, on the utmost heights of Mount Zaphon.
> [14] I will ascend above the tops of the clouds; I will make myself like the Most High."
> [15] But you are brought down to the realm of the dead, to the depths of the pit.

---

[105] Arnold, Clinton E.; Exegetical Commentary On The New Testament: Ephesians. Grand Rapids, MI. Zondervan pg. 219

[16] Those who see you stare at you, they ponder your fate: "Is this the man who shook the earth and made kingdoms tremble,

[17]the man who made the world a wilderness, who overthrew its cities and would not let his captives go home?"

[18] All the kings of the nations lie in state, each in his own tomb.

[19] But you are cast out of your tomb like a rejected branch; you are covered with the slain, with those pierced by the sword, those who descend to the stones of the pit. Like a corpse trampled underfoot,

This set of verses shows that God has overcome in the Spiritual realm and in the Cosmos. To see God's power in application in the physical realm we need to look just after the day of Pentecost in the book of Acts.

Acts 3:1-9
KJV
[1] Now Peter and John went up together into the temple at the hour of prayer, being the ninth hour.

[2] And a certain man lame from his mother's womb was carried, whom they laid daily at the gate of the temple which is called Beautiful, to ask alms of them that entered into the temple;

[3] Who seeing Peter and John about to go into the temple asked an alms.

[4] And Peter, fastening his eyes upon him with John, said, Look on us.

[5] And he gave heed unto them, expecting to receive something of them.

[6] Then Peter said, Silver and gold have I none; but such as I have give I thee: In the name of Jesus Christ of Nazareth rise up and walk.

[7] And he took him by the right hand, and lifted him up: and immediately his feet and ankle bones received strength.

[8] And he leaping up stood, and walked, and entered with them into the temple, walking, and leaping, and praising God.

[9] And all the people saw him walking and praising God:

This brings us to the conclusion of the expanded translation of this important verse. Both of these expanded translations really fall short of communicating the greatness inside of this verse.

Ephesians 3:20
Expanded Version
[20] Now to Him who is able and ready to perform exceedingly abundantly above all that we ask or can conceptualize. All this is in accordance with the Power of God, which worketh in us

OR

Ephesians 3:20
Expanded Version #2
[20] Now to God, who is able and ready to perform on behalf of His people, exceeding far more abundantly than we can think, or conceptualize, in the spiritual realm, in the cosmos, and in the earthly places. All this strength is utilized in accordance with the power of God who worketh in us

These seem to be the some of the strongest verses in the Bible concerning the individual's standing with believing. No other verse brings the three powers together in one and then shows the activation of these verses by believing as the fullness of the Godhead bodily dwells within the individual. δύναμαι is the active use of the power, δύναμις, is the noun which is the surplus power, held in reserve for use when the need exceeds the power that God is currently exerted and ἐνεργέω is the energy of all the power. This power can be thought of as the amperage of the power, while the wattage and voltage come through the other powers. This verse demonstrates that God is not separated from His people in any way, but rather He abides within them and is able and ready to take care of the needs of His people. God is the eternal resource for His children. This verse should be considered to be the apex of not only the Great Prayer of Ephesians but the complete and total apex of the epistle to the Ephesians.

Ephesians 3:21

Ephesians 3:21
KJV
[21] Unto him be glory in the church by Christ Jesus throughout all ages, world without end. Amen.

Ephesians 3:21
RSV
[21] to him be glory in the church and in Christ Jesus to all generations, for ever and ever. Amen.

Ephesians 3:21
Aramaic Peshitta Version
[21] to him [be] glory in his church by Yeshue-Meshikha in all generations, forever and ever. Amen

Ephesians 3:21
New International Version
[21] to him be glory in the church and in Christ Jesus throughout all generations, for ever and ever! Amen.

Ephesians 3:21
Darby Translation
[21] to him be glory in the assembly in Christ Jesus unto all generations of `the age of ages. Amen).

Ephesians 3:21
Wycliffe/Tyndale Ploughboy Translation
[21] to him be glory in the church, and in Christ Jesus, into all the generations of the world of worlds [into all the generations of the worlds of worlds]. Amen.

This verse along with the previous verse, make up the doxology of this prayer. Verse 20 shows the abilities the God has, which He intends to be used for His creative works, including His children, while verse 21 brings in the glory to God and the "length" that the glory is deserved for. The glory is also to be found "in the church".

The true purpose of this church is the ascription of "glory" to God. The equivalent of "glory" could also be "honor", greatness" or power". Glory has with it an attribute of "illusion[106] of greatness" a "brightness of light". We see in the book of Acts how Herod attempted a counterfeit of glory.

> Acts 12:21
> KJV
> [21] And upon a set day Herod, arrayed in royal apparel, sat upon his throne, and made an oration unto them.
> [22] And the people gave a shout, saying, It is the voice of a god, and not of a man.
> [23] And immediately the angel of the Lord smote him, because he gave not God the glory: and he was eaten of worms, and gave up the ghost.
> [24] But the word of God grew and multiplied.

The Royal Apparel that Herod wore that day made of a thin silver cloth that shone brightly in the sun, hence this is the reason the people said it was the voice of a god and not of a man. The record from Josephus is as follows:

> 21. Now, when Agrippa had reigned three years over all Judea, he came to the city Cesarea, which was formerly called *Strato's Tower*; and there he exhibited shows in honour of Caesar, upon his being informed that there was a certain festival celebrated to make vows for his safety. At which festival, a great multitude was gotten together of the principal persons, and such as were of dignity through his province. On the second day of which shows he put on a garment made wholly of silver, and of a contexture truly wonderful, and came into the theatre early in the morning;

---

[106] Illusion is an illumination of light. This is different than the trick of a magician.

at which time the silver of his garment, being illuminated by the fresh reflection of the sun's rays upon it, shone out after a surprising manner, and was so resplendent as to spread an horror over those that looked intently upon him; and presently his flatterers cried out, one from one place, and another from another, (though not for his good), That "he was a god;" and they added, "Be thou merciful to us; for although we have hitherto reverenced thee only as a man, yet shall we henceforth own thee as superior to mortal nature." Upon this the king did neither rebuke them, nor reject their impious flattery. But as he presently afterward looked up, he saw an owl (22) sitting on a certain rope over his head, and immediately understood that this bird was the messenger of ill tidings, as it had once been the messenger of good tidings to him; and fell into the deepest sorrow. A severe pain also arose in his belly and began in a most violent manner. He therefore looked upon his friends, and said, "I, whom you call a *god*, am commanded presently to depart this life; while Providence thus reproves the lying words you just now said to me; and I, who was by you called *immortal*, am immediately to be hurried away by death. But I am bound to accept of what Providence allots, as it pleases God; for we have by no means lived ill, but in a splendid and happy manner." When he said this, his pain was become violent. Accordingly he was carried into the palace; and the rumor went abroad everywhere, that he would certainly die in a little time. But the multitude presently sat in sackcloth, with their wives and children, after the law of their country, and besought God for the king's recovery. All places were also full of mourning and lamentation. Now the king rested in an high chamber, and as he saw them below lying prostrate on the ground, he could not himself forbear weeping. And, when he had been quite worn out by the pain in his belly for five days, he departed this life, being in the fifty fourth year of his age[107]

The attempt by Herod to usurp glory that was to be only presented to God was the reason for his demise. Jesus Christ is the mediator of

---

[107] Josephus, Antiquities Book XIX. viii. 2

the glory that we give to God, as we are in Christ Jesus. The believers who are incorporated into the body of Christ give Glory to God. Jesus Christ is the mediator of God's activity toward us and the mediator of our response to praise of the Father. Our thanksgiving to God can only be given in the name of Jesus Christ. So also glory can be ascribed to God only within the realm of Christ Jesus.[108]

The Puritan Exposition on Ephesians marks three items that must be shown in the conclusion[109]:

The Conclusion of the Prayer

1. The Persons Praising
2. The Mediator in Whom
3. The Durance

The book also discusses two separate doctrinal points in the verse. The first lets us see who they are in whom God is truly praised, who are the true members of the church. This looks to be very far from the truth, as it does not touch the whole idea of grace and not of works. Ephesians spells this out previously:

> Ephesians 2:9
> KJV
> [9] Not of works, lest any man should boast.

> Ephesians 2:8,9
> RSV
> [8] For by grace you have been saved through faith; and this is not your own doing, it is the gift of God --
> [9] not because of works, lest any man should boast.

---

[108] O'Brien, Peter T.; The Letter To The Ephesians. Grand Rapids, MI. Wm B. Eerdmans Publishing Co. pg. 269

[109] Goodwin, Thomas and Bayne, Paul., Puritan Exposition Of Ephesians. Sovereign Grace Book Club Book II Pg. 210

The Puritans also talk about "acceptable" praise to Him[110]. This comes from the same idea of Cain and Abel:

> Hebrews 11:4
> RSV
> [4] By faith Abel offered to God a more **acceptable** sacrifice than Cain, through which he received approval as righteous, God bearing witness by accepting his gifts; he died, but through his faith he is still speaking.

It is not man who determines the quality of the sacrifice, but rather God is the only judge. When one is born again of God's spirit, he immediately becomes a member of the true church. There is no waiting at the gate to become accepted in the beloved. It is an immediate acceptance, without any further qualification.

The second doctrinal point that the Puritans give is "This is the last circumstance of time, as it doth teach us the large hearts we should have toward God's glory. So, it doth assure us that God will in all ages have a people which will praise him; Hell gates i.e. all the powers of darkness, 'shall not subvert His church'. The use of this is in regard to the comfort of His people; it assures us that that though hell should break loose, Yet God will still have His people. For the words are as much affirmative as optative[111], they do tell us as well what shall be, as wish that it should be[112]"

Several of the doxologies that are found in the New Testament speak of Jesus Christ bringing glory δόζα to the father[113], almost in a sense as if Jesus Christ is working in his function as a mediator between God and man.

---

[110] Ibid

[111] The optative mood is a grammatical mood that expresses a wish. It is extremely close to the cohortative mood when used as a hopeful statement and almost identical to the subjunctive mood in a grammatical sense.

[112] Ibid Vol II pg. 211

[113] Romans 16:27; I Peter 4:11

II Timothy 2:5
KJV
[5] For there is one God, and one **mediator** between God and men, the man Christ Jesus;

Hebrews 9:15
KJV
[15] And for this cause he is the **mediator** of the new testament, that by means of death, for the redemption of the transgressions that were under the first testament, they which are called might receive the promise of eternal inheritance.

This appears to be the only doxology in which bringing glory to God is the primary purpose and principal intention of the church.

It is the object and intention of the church to bring glory to God forever. Considering that at the very core of the church is the great Musterion, for the bringing together in one all the believers.

Ephesians 3:6
RSV
[6] that is, how the Gentiles are fellow heirs, members of the same body, and partakers of the promise in Christ Jesus through the gospel.

Ephesians 3:6
KJV
[6] That the Gentiles should be fellowheirs, and of the same body, and partakers of his promise in Christ by the gospel:

The breaking down the barriers between Jew and Gentile was not only for the idea of one body, but it is what that one body stands for, one body, fellowheirs, partakers of His promise in Christ Jesus. This is in the immediate; all the promises available to man in the New Testament are available to both Jew and Gentile as they are now both one and neither has the title of Jew or Gentile. In the future we have the promise of both receiving the heavenly reward. We will forever be with him, seated at the right hand of God. We inherit heaven.

Arnold brings up a very interesting translation of the second section of this verse. εἰς πάσας τὰς γενεὰς τοῦ αἰῶνος τῶν αἰώνως which could read "for all the generations of the age of the ages"[114] Paul's addition of the word "generations" seems to not be of any great relevance since within the prayer it speaks of the church as one. such as "of whom the whole family", "comprehend with all saints", What is of note is the fact that Paul uses the repetition of the plural forms of age "αἰῶνος" (ages of ages), from which get the word "forever".[115] We could literally translate this phrase as "for all the generations of the age of ages". If we look at this verse in light of its translations, we have to see that Paul's addition of the word "generations" is a section of time, plural. Next his use of the "age of ages" brings us to a point of endless time. Part one of the verse "unto him be glory in the church" we now add the time component of the verse and see that God is deserving of our praise for millions upon millions of years to come.

The third section of the Great Prayer beginning with "that ye may be filled with all the fulness of God" can rightfully be called "the climax petition". Paul has no intention of saying that any one believer or all the believers combined could ever contain all the fulness of God. The word "unto" is indicative of a standard or oft times a goal to be reached. In this verse the standard would be the glory due Him and that glory is church wide throughout all ages. It is only fitting that all glory be to God. Every member of the family of God is conceived as having all the fulness of God inherent within him or her. This can be from one perspective as true because whatever the need is, God will supply.

---

[114] Arnold, Clinton E.; Exegetical Commentary On The New Testament: Ephesians. Grand Rapids, MI. Zondervan pg. 220
[115] We also derive the figure of speech Repetitio from this plural use of the word.

Philippians 4:19
KJV
[19] But my God shall supply all your need according to
his riches in glory by Christ Jesus.

Though the believer may not actually have the object of necessity at the
time, God is willing and able to provide a constant supply

There are several doxologies presented by Paul in his writings. Matching
the doxologies against each other is also evidence against the Deutero-
Pauline concept. The following chart is representative of the doxologies
that Paul presents in the prayers of the epistles that he wrote.

New Testament Doxologies of Paul

Romans 1:25	[25]The Creator who is blessed forever
Romans 9:5	[5] Christ who is over all, God blessed forever
Romans 11:33-36	[33]O the depth of the riches both of the wisdom and knowledge of God! how unsearchable are his judgments, and his ways past finding out!
	[34] For who hath known the mind of the Lord? Or who hath been his counselor?
	[35] Or who hath first given to him, and it shall be recompensed unto him again?
	[36] For of him, and through him, and to him, are all things: to whom be glory for ever. Amen.
Romans 16:27	[27] To God only wise, be glory through Jesus Christ for ever. Amen.
II Corinthians 1:3,4	Blessed be God.... who comforteth us
II Corinthians 11:31	[31] The God and Father of our Lord Jesus Christ, which is blessed for evermore, knoweth that I lie not.
Ephesians 1:3	[3]Blessed Be the God and Father of our Lord Jesus Christ. Who hath blessed us
Ephesians 3:21	[21] Unto him be glory in the church by Christ Jesus throughout all ages, world without end. Amen.
I Timothy 1:17	[17] Now unto the King eternal, immortal, invisible, the only wise God, be honour and glory for ever and ever. Amen.
I Timothy 6:15,16	[15] Which in his times he shall shew, who is the blessed and only Potentate, the King of kings, and Lord of lords;
	[16] Who only hath immortality, dwelling in the light which no man can approach unto; whom no man hath seen, nor can see: to whom be honour and power everlasting. Amen.

Hebrews 13:20,21[116] [20] Now the God of peace, that brought again from the dead our Lord Jesus, that great shepherd of the sheep, through the blood of the everlasting covenant,

[21] Make you perfect in every good work to do his will, working in you that which is well pleasing in his sight, through Jesus Christ; to whom be glory for ever and ever. Amen.

Eleven of these Doxologies take into account a time period. The two that do not are from the beginning passages of the epistle sin which they are written. This particular doxology in Ephesians is unique, in that it envisions the generations or times to come. Paul's prison epistles speak of differing time periods referred to by the doxologies[117]. It is important to note the time period of the doxologies in order to know all the parties to whom the writing of the epistle is referring. For example, Colossians 1:26, the epistle mentions the believers of previous times (prior to the Grace Administration) and also the believers in the current Grace Administration. Of the eight that bring in periods of time all bring in forever, meaning into the future dispensations.

Time periods of Doxologies

1. Past Generations:
   Ephesians 3:5
   KJV
   [5] Which in other ages was not made known unto the sons of men, as it is now revealed unto his holy apostles and prophets by the Spirit;

---

[116] A Pauline authorship is in question concerning Hebrews.
[117] Welch, Charles H.; In Heavenly Places. London, The Berea Publishing Trust pg.322

Colossians 1:26
KJV
[26] Even the mystery which hath been hid from ages and from generations, but now is made manifest to his saints:

2. Present Generation
Philippians 2:15
KJV
[15] That ye may be blameless and harmless, the sons of God, without rebuke, in the midst of a crooked and perverse nation, among whom ye shine as lights in the world;

3. Future Generation
Ephesians 3:21
KJV
[21] Unto him be glory in the church by Christ Jesus throughout all ages, world without end. Amen.

I Timothy 1:17
KJV
[17] Now unto the King eternal, immortal, invisible, the only wise God, be honour and glory for ever and ever. Amen.

From a dispensational viewpoint, knowing the time period to which something is addressed is paramount to the study of the scriptures. For example, before the day of Pentecost there were no Christians. The opportunity to become a Christian was not available until the day.

A few of the doxologies of the New Testament concern Jesus Christ bringing glory to God the Father, however Ephesians 3:21 is the only doxology which refers to the church as the medium in which the glory is given. The church is God's masterpiece, and the very existence of the church is a vehicle in which true glory is presented to God. We see from this verse that both the church and Jesus Christ will bring glory to God eternally, εἰς πάσας τὰς γενεὰς τοῦ αἰῶνος τῶν αἰώνων. The most common way of saying forever in the text is to use two plural forms of age τοῦ αἰῶνος τῶν αἰώνων. This phrase is also often translated as "forever and ever".

A question arises whether there is any significance to the fact that Paul uses "generation" and a singular form of "age" in some early occurrences of this time. Others in the Old Testament had also used this occasionally, and it is also used in the apocryphal writings[118].

In most writings it simply means forever, as without an ending. This is much different than τελός which, has a definitive ending point. This is the absolute end point of a timeline.

One thing that needs to be considered is whether or not verse 20 is a parembole or a logical progression of the Prayer. It appears that verse 20 is a further explanation by way of insertion. Looking at the prayer without verse 20 it still maintains its flow.

> Ephesians 3:18,19,21
> RSV
> [18] may have power to comprehend with all the saints what is the breadth and length and height and depth,
> [19] and to know the love of Christ which surpasses knowledge, that you may be filled with all the fulness of God.
> [21] to him be glory in the church and in Christ Jesus to all generations, for ever and ever. Amen.
>
> Ephesians 3:18,19,21
> KJV
> [18] May be able to comprehend with all saints what is the breadth, and length, and depth, and height;

---

[118] Tobias 1:4;14:5; and others

[19] And to know the love of Christ, which passeth knowledge, that ye might be filled with all the fulness of God.

[21] Unto him be glory in the church by Christ Jesus throughout all ages, world without end. Amen.

Since the passages flow well without the inclusion of verse 20, we can safely assume that it is a figure of speech of a Parembole[119]. It is also another very rarely used figure of speech called a Characterismos (χαρακτηπισμός) which is a description of the morals or the character of a person.[120] It is also the designation by a characteristic marking.

"Unto him be glory in the church" seems to show quite a similarity to Ephesians 3:10

Ephesians 3:10
KJV
[10] To the intent that now unto the principalities and powers in heavenly places might be known by the church the manifold wisdom of God,

The manifold (or variagated) wisdom of God is the basis for this request of prayer. This manifold wisdom of God is in line with "exceeding abundantly above all that we ask or think".

ἀμήν is a word used constantly in Christendom yet is probably the least understood. It is used at the end of songs and at the prayers and is thought to mean simply "the end". When the word is sung it uses a short "a". When it is spoken at the end of a prayer it is a long "A". In the Old Testament (LXX) the word ἀμήν was by individuals and groups of Jews to confirm the acceptance of a certain jobs that were given to certain

---

[119] A further description by way of insertion.

[120] Bullinger, E.W.; Figures of Speech Used In The Bible, Ann Arbor Michigan, Baker Book House Company pg. 448. Bullinger does not list any uses of this figure of speech in the Bible.

men, which were considered to be tasks that needed to be performed by the will of God.

> I Kings 1:36
> KJV
> [36] And Benaiah the son of Jehoiada answered the king, and said, Amen: the LORD God of my lord the king say so too (ἀμήν).

It is very interesting to see that this word was used in the Old Testament times for both blessings and curses. In the New Testament times we see it used almost always in a very positive light. In the Old Testament we see it used to confirm a personal rendering of a curse or divine threat.

In the Old Testament times we also see it used in a positive sense where it confirms or adds a seal to a doxology that gives praise to God. In Judaism the use of ἀμήν is widespread and firmly established. A very great value is added to its utterance as it gives certification to that which was just spoken. In synagogue worship (but not in Temple worship) it occurs as the response of the community to the detailed praise, which the priest uttered with the prayers he spoke. It occurred in the synagogue also at the end of each of the three sections of the Aaronic blessing, It was spoken by a different priest each section

> Numbers 6:22ff
> RSV
> [22] The LORD said to Moses,
> [23] "Say to Aaron and his sons, Thus you shall bless the people of Israel: you shall say to them,
> [24] The LORD bless you and keep you:
> [25] The LORD make his face to shine upon you, and be gracious to you:
> [26] The LORD lift up his countenance upon you, and give you peace.
> [27] "So shall they put my name upon the people of Israel, and I will bless them."

This Aaronic blessing was a confession of praise to God, which was set before the people and which the community of the people was told to make operative by the affirmation of ἀμήν at the conclusion of each of the three sections. When a vow was made saying ἀμήν to it meant that there was a full and complete intention to engage and complete the vow.

> Ecclesiastes 5:4
> KJV
> [4] When thou vowest a vow unto God, defer not to pay it; for he hath no pleasure in fools: pay that which thou hast vowed.

Kittel's says speaking "Amen" to a curse implied either the cursing of another person or placing oneself under a curse. The same is true of Amen to a blessing. The word can be shifted to either blessing or cursing. There are also a number of times were amen is used to designate a concluding wish at the end of ones own prayers. In these cases it is not so much a confirmation of what was spoken but rather hope for what is desired[121].

> I Samuel 1:8-20
> KJV
> [8] Then said Elkanah her husband to her, Hannah, why weepest thou? and why eatest thou not? and why is thy heart grieved? am not I better to thee than ten sons?
> [9] So Hannah rose up after they had eaten in Shiloh, and after they had drunk. Now Eli the priest sat upon a seat by a post of the temple of the LORD.
> [10] And she was in bitterness of soul, and prayed unto the LORD, and wept sore.
> [11] And she vowed a vow, and said, O LORD of hosts, if thou wilt indeed look on the affliction of thine handmaid, and remember me, and not forget thine handmaid, but wilt give unto thine handmaid a man

---

[121] Ibid

child, then I will give him unto the LORD all the days of his life, and there shall no razor come upon his head.

[12] And it came to pass, as she continued praying before the LORD, that Eli marked her mouth.

[13] Now Hannah, she spake in her heart; only her lips moved, but her voice was not heard: therefore Eli thought she had been drunken.

[14] And Eli said unto her, How long wilt thou be drunken? put away thy wine from thee.

[15] And Hannah answered and said, No, my lord, I am a woman of a sorrowful spirit: I have drunk neither wine nor strong drink, but have poured out my soul before the LORD.

[16] Count not thine handmaid for a daughter of Belial: for out of the abundance of my complaint and grief have I spoken hitherto.

[17] Then Eli answered and said, Go in peace: and the God of Israel grant thee thy petition that thou hast asked of him.

[18] And she said, Let thine handmaid find grace in thy sight. So the woman went her way, and did eat, and her countenance was no more sad.

[19] And they rose up in the morning early, and worshipped before the LORD, and returned, and came to their house to Ramah: and Elkanah knew Hannah his wife; and the LORD remembered her.

[20] Wherefore it came to pass, when the time was come about after Hannah had conceived, that she bare a son, and called his name Samuel, saying, Because I have asked him of the LORD.

There are three verses in the New Testament that testify to the original meaning of the word ἀμήν. In Revelation 1:7, it is used along with ναὶ or "yes".

Revelation 1:7
KJV
[7] Behold, he cometh with clouds; and every eye shall see him, and they also which pierced him: and all kindreds of the earth shall wail because of him. Even so (ναί) Amen.

in Revelation 22:20 it is shown as the answer of the ἐκκλησία to the divine yes. The Yes here does not bring in an eschatological petition but rather it acknowledges the divine promise made by God. The divine yes by God is acknowledged by the ἀμήν of the church.

Revelation 22:20
KJV
[20] He which testifieth these things saith, Surely I come quickly. Amen. Even so, (ναι) come, Lord Jesus.

Also in Revelation 3:14 Christ by himself can be referred to as the ὁ ἀμήν which means he himself is the affirmative response to the divine yes in him. When the strength of the passage is considered, it is seen that this is not a figure of speech though it appears as such.

Revelation 3:14
KJV
[14] And unto the angel of the church of the Laodiceans write; These things saith the Amen, the faithful and true witness, the beginning of the creation of God;

Taking into account any figures of speech, the construction of the prayer as a whole, the uniqueness of translations in their specific use and usages the final verse of the doxology is translated as an Expanded Translation as such:

Ephesians 3:21
Expanded Version
[21] Unto God be all glory given in the church by Jesus Christ, throughout all time, ages and generations, forever and ever. Amen

Conclusion

The Great Prayer of Ephesians, on behalf of all Christians is the most important prayer ever written and spoken for the church. As a literary work, it is written perfectly in its construction, scope, and rendering. No other work has ever been written that portrays the very heart of God so wonderfully as to unfold the greatness of His love to the church of God and to each individual within the named church. The Great Prayer is instructional for all believers as to their responsibility to render all glory and praise to the Father.

Ephesians is the apex of all revelation to the Church of God. As Appendix B points out, the epistle is perfectly balanced with seven doctrinal and seven practical treatises. The Great Prayer is the center of the epistle upon which all fourteen treatises hang. The prayer is the bridge between the doctrine and practical. The doxology of the prayer is descriptive of the power of God and how the power is purposed. It also tells us of the responsibility of each believer to give all praise and glory to God, the Father of us all.

The writing of the great prayer is very uniquely Pauline. With the beginning utilizing both address and a doxology (glorification), and a doxology as a finish to the prayer, the construction seems to solve the question as to whether this is a Deutero-Pauline authorship or was it written by Paul.

Very simply the prayer is of an Introversion construction:

The Great Prayer of Ephesians

Introversion

A. Address and Glorification Eph. 3:14,15
     B. Intercession #1 on behalf of the saints - Establishment Eph 3:16,17
    B. Intercession #2 on behalf of the saints – Practical Eph. 3:18,19
A. Doxology Eph. 3:20,21

The prayer is very elegant in its presentation to all the members of the Body of Christ. By this prayer all the workings of the gift of holy spirit within are energized. We learn through this prayer that all of God's power is available to us who believe. All this power becomes as a result of the intercessions of this prayer that are presented to God. The great prayer ends with voice of a client shouting the greatness of his Patron and the time of his life. The prayer is the spark that ignites the greatness of power inherent in the epistle to the Ephesians. Both the Old Testament and the New Testament have prayers in them that could be called Great Prayers. For the New Testament, it is the prayer in Ephesians, while Job has a Great Prayer in the Old Testament The Lord's Prayer is not put into this category. Just standing alone it is a tremendous prayer, it is considered to be an Instructional prayer as it is used to teach the people "how to pray".

Prayers cover different situations in life. I Thessalonians 5 tell us the types of prayers we should be doing in our everyday lives:

> I Thessalonians 5:16-18
> KJV
> [16] Rejoice evermore.
> [17] Pray without ceasing.
> [18] In everything give thanks: for this is the will of God in Christ Jesus concerning you.

Giving of thanks to God is what we are on this earth for. We are designed to receive from God and to be thankful to Him for all our blessings. When looking at prayers that the Father asks of the believers one needs to carefully consider I Timothy as God states here what makes up a prayer, a description of what it is and what it is not.

I Timothy 2:1-3
KJV
[1] I exhort therefore, that, first of all, supplications, prayers, intercessions, and giving of thanks, be made for all men;
[2] For kings, and for all that are in authority; that we may lead a quiet and peaceable life in all godliness and honesty.
[3] For this is good and acceptable in the sight of God our Saviour;

Appendix A

The Structure of Ephesians

Ephesians

Introversion

A| Opening – called Salutation 1:1,2

    B| All Spiritual Blessings 1:3-14

        C| Prayer to God by Paul 1:15-23

            D| Seated in the Heavenlies 2:1-7

                E| God's Works 2:8-10

                    F| New Man 2:11-18

                        G| The Temple fitly framed 2:19-22

                        H| The Mystery 3:1-13

                        I| Prayer 3:14-21

                        H| The One Body 4:1-6

                      G| The Body fitly joined 4:7-16

                    F| Putting on the New Man 4:17-32

                E| Mans Works 5:1-6,9

            D| Standing in the Heavenlies 6:10-18

        C| Prayer to God for All 6:19,20

    B| Making Known the Spiritual Blessings 6:21,22

A| The Close – called Benediction 6:23,24

Appendix B

P46

Written between 100-250AD, we can consider p46 to be the oldest known MSS of Ephesians in existence. P46 appears to be 95% complete with some deterioration in the lower left corner and the bottom of the papyri[122]. The scribe used several abbreviations, for example πρα for πατρια and χρυ for χπιστοζ. This MSS is in a codex form[123]

---

[122] There is also deterioration along the left side and the top however this does not affect the readability of the MSS.

[123] "Image reproduced courtesy of the Michigan Papyrology Collection."

The scribe who wrote this is unknown and the manner in which he came to write this Codex is also unknown. It could have been written as part of a larger consortium such as in a scriptorium. Evidence points to it being a one- on -one writing. There is only one copy of the MSS known to exist therefore the chances of a Scriptorium being used to write the MSS are very slim. Ephesians is located in Folio 70-85, the text type is Alexandrian. The size of the MSS is 28cm*16cm and the width of the text is approx. 11cm. There are seven leaves missing from the codex. This is enough to contain II Thessalonians and Philemon. This is considered to be the first MSS with sense markings, which are somewhat similar to verse markings. The Nomina Sacra dates the MSS at 175-225 AD. At present, the University of Michigan owns half of the MSS and the Chester Beatty Library in Ireland owns the other half. Kurt Aland placed P46 in Category 1 text as an Alexandrian Text. Stichometric notes can be found throughout the P46 codex. They appear at the end of each epistle, noting the number of lines that the previous epistle contained. This was a way for the bookmaker to keep track of how many lines of text the scribe had written (and thus how much to charge for the codex). It is interesting to note that throughout this codex, the number of lines reported for each epistle is higher than the number of lines reported in other copies of the same text. This may suggest that someone was padding the numbers in order to charge more money[124] P46 is by far the best preserved MSS which contains the entire epistle to the Ephesians that is readable while others, such as p99 are more than 50% unreadable.

The MSS p46 is translated into English as follows[125]:

"Of this by reason of I bend the knees of mine unto the father of who all lineage in heaven and on earth takes name that he may give according to the riches glory of him power to become mighty through the spirit of him in the inward man that dwelling of Christ through faith in hearts of your in love rooted and founded that you have strength to lay hold of all the holy ones what is the breadth and depth [The next

---

[124] http://www.lib.umich.edu/reading/Paul/stichometry.html
[125] Section 151; Verso/ Size 15.2 x 22.3 cm / Inventory # Pumicing 6238

portion is unreadable] and to know the exceeding knowledgeable love of Christ so that you will be filled to all the fullness of God now to one empowered beyond all things to do over abundantly we inquire or we think according to power operating in us glory in the church also [the rest of the leaf is unreadable]"

Appendix C

Expanded Translation of Ephesians 3:14-21

These expanded translations of the verses are meant to give another point of reference to the reader based upon the research found in each verse. Wherever possible language construction and figures of speech are present as they are in the Codex Receptus. The research in each section attempts to give the reader what is considered in each of the Expanded Versions.

[14] For this reason (as I spoke afore) I bow my knees in thankfulness and humility to God, The Father.

[15] For whom the whole family, both on the Earth and in the Heavenlies is named.

[16] That the Father of us all, will give unto you, in accordance with the unquantifiable riches of his glory, strength, with his great might, by his gift of holy spirit in your innermost being

[17] So that Christ, The only begotten of the Father will dwell in your hearts by the faith you have demonstrated; that you, who being rooted as a tree and founded as a building in love,

[18] May be able as a direct result of the holy spirit that resides in you, be able to understand with all the saints what is the breadth which extends to all races and peoples and the length which spans from eternity to everlasting, and the depth that is so low no part of the

creation can ascertain it, and the height that is far above all principalities leading to the very right hand of God

[19] And to experience the tranquility of the love of Christ which is far beyond knowledge, that your life will become one of being filled and overflowing with the fulness of our Fathers love

[20] Now to Him who is able and ready to perform exceedingly abundantly above all that we ask or can conceptualize. All this is in accordance with the Power of God, which worketh in us

OR
Ephesians 3:20 alternate reading

Expanded Version #2

[20] Now to God, who is able and ready to perform on behalf of His people, exceeding far more abundantly than we can think, or conceptualize, in the spiritual realm, in the cosmos, and in the earthly places. All this strength is utilized in accordance with the power of God who worketh in us

[21] Unto God be all glory given in the church by Jesus Christ, throughout all ages, time and generations, forever and ever. Amen

Bibliography

Abissi Jr, Frank.; The Doctrine of Ephesians, A Philological Examination. Grand Rapids, MI. Outskirts Press 2015

Abissi Jr, Frank,; A Reexamination of the Lordship of Jesus Christ, Patronage. Grand Rapids, MI. XLibris 2017

Aland, Kurt; Black, Matthew' Martini, Carlo M.; Metzger, Bruce M.; Wikgren, Allen; The Greek New Testament: West Germany, The United Bible Societies, 1975

Arnold, Clinton E.; Exegetical Commentary On The New Testament: Ephesians. Grand Rapids, MI. Zondervan 2010

Barth, Markus; The Anchor Bible: Ephesians 1-3, Garden City, New York. Doubleday and Company 1974

John Bengal Edited by Rev. W.L. Blackley M.A. and Rev. James Hawes, M.A.; The Critical English New Testament in Three Volumes: Commentary on the Entire New Testament, London: Daldy, Isbister & Co. 56 Ludgate Hill 1876

John Bengal Edited by Rev. W.L. Blackley M.A. and Rev. James Hawes, M.A. The Gnomon of the New Testament: London: Daldy, Isbister & Co 56 Ludgate Hill 1876

Berkhof, Louis: Introduction to the New Testament, Oxford, Benediction Classics, 2009

Betz, Hans Dieter; The Greek Magical Papyri in Translation Including the Demotic Spells. Chicago and London, The University of Chicago Press 1986.

Borgen, Peder; Fuglseth, Kare., and Skarsten, Roald.: The Philo Index; Grand Rapids, MI. Wm. B. Eerdmans Publishing Co. 2000

Bromily, Geoffrey W., Gerhard Kittel and Gerhard Friedrich, Editors.: Theological Dictionary Of The New Testament Abridged in One Volume; Grand Rapids, MI. Wm B. Eerdmans Publishing Company, The Paternoster Press. 1985

Bruce, F.F.: A new Presentation of his Classic The Epistle to the Ephesians a Verse by verse Exposition.; 2012 Bath, UK

Bruce, F.F.: The New International Commentary on The New Testament: The Epistles to the Colossians, To Philemon, and to the Ephesians: Grand Rapids, MI. Wm. B. Eerdmans Publishing 1984.

Bullinger, E.W.: The Companion Bible. Grand Rapids, MI. Zondervan Bible Publishers. 1974

Bullinger, Ethelbert W. A Critical Lexicon and Concordance to the English and Greek New Testament., Grand Rapids, MI 49506, Zondervan Publishing House, 1979

Bullinger, E.W.; Figures of Speech Used In The Bible, Ann Arbor Michigan, Baker Book House Company 1968

Bullinger, E.W.: Number In Scripture, Grand Rapids, MI. Kregel Publications. No Copyright.

Bullinger, E.W.; The Church Epistles:... Decatur, MI. Invictus. No Copyright.

Bullinger, E.W.; The Prayers of Ephesians:. Decatur, MI Invictus. No Copyright.

Eadie, John., Commentary On The Epistle To The Ephesians, Minneapolis, Minnesota. James and Klock Christian Publishing Co, 1883 reprinted 1977

Edersheim, Alfred: The Life And Times Of Jesus The Messiah, Grand Rapids, Wm.B. Eerdmans Publishing Co. 1971

Freeman, James M. Manners and Customs of the Bible, Plainfield, New Jersey, Logos International 1972

Goodwin, Thomas and Bayne, Paul., Puritan Exposition Of Ephesians. Sovereign Grace Book Club 1958

Hatch, Edwin and Redpath, Henry A., A Concordance of the Septuagint and other Greek versions of the Old Testament including the Apocryphal Books. In Two Volumes.; Grand Rapids, MI Baker Book House1983

Keener, Craig, The IVP Bible Background Commentary (New Testament) 1993 Downers Grove, IL, Intervarsity Press, 60515-1426 1993

Kittel, Gerhard: Theological Dictionary Of The New Testament. Grand Rapids, MI. Wm. B. Eerdmans Publishing Company. 1964, Ten Volumes

Lamsa, Dr. George M.: Gospel Light. Covington, Georgia. The Aramaic Bible Society 1999

Lamsa, George M. The Holy Bible from Ancient Eastern Manuscripts, Nashville, Holman Bible Publishers, 1957

Longman, Tremper III and Garland, David E.: The Expositor's Bible Commentary Revised Edition, Ephesians – Philemon, Grand Rapids, MI 2006

MacArthur, John Jr.: The MacArthur New Testament Commentary Ephesians, Chicago, The Moody Bible Institute of Chicago 1986

Magiera, Janet M.: Aramaic Peshitta New Testament Translation. Truth or Consequences, New Mexico. LWM Publications 2006

Marshall, Alfred: The Interlinear KJV-NIV Parallel New Testament In Greek and English. Grand Rapids, MI, Zondervan Publishing House. 1975

Marshall, Howard I., Travis, Stephen., Paul Ian.: Exploring The New Testament, A Guide to the Letters and Revelation, Downers Grove, IL. InterVarsity Press. 2002

Metzger, Bruce M. A Textual Commentary On The Greek New Testament. London-New York, United Bible Societies 1971

Morrish, George; A Concordance of the Septuagint. Grand Rapids, MI. Zondervan Publishing House. 1976

Moulton, Harold K. The Analytical Greek Lexicon revised 1978 Edition, Grand Rapids, MI. The Zondervan Corporation 1978

Nestle-Aland: Novum Testamentum Graece 27th revised edition, 9th corrected printing. Peabody, MA, Hendrickson Publishers 2006

O'Brien, Peter T.; The Letter To The Ephesians. Grand Rapids, MI. Wm B. Eerdmans Publishing Co. 1999

Septuagint Version of the Old Testament: Grand Rapids, MI. Zondervan Publishing House. 1970

Snodgrass, Klyne Ryland., Stories with intent : a Comprehensive Guide to the Parables of Jesus. Grand Rapids, MI Wm. B. Eerdmans Publishing Co. 2015

Stott, John; God's New Society: The Message of Ephesians (Bible Speaks Today). Downers Grove, IL. The Intervarsity Press 1980.

Strong, James; The Exhaustive Concordance of the Bible. McLean, Virginia. Mac Donald Publishing Co.

Welch, Charles H.; In Heavenly Places. London, The Berea Publishing Trust Unknown Date.

Whiston, William; Josephus - Complete Works. Grand Rapids, MI. Kregel Publications 1981.

Young, Robert LL.D.: Analytical Concordance to the Bible; Grand Rapids, MI. Wm B. Eerdmans Publishing Co. 1970

Internet resources

http://quod.lib.umich.edu **The King James Version, University of Michigan**

http://quod.lib.umich.edu **The Revised Standard Version, University of Michigan**

http://www.perseus.tufts.edu **Plato and Homer, Heraclitus**

https://www.biblegateway.com/passage **Bible gateway**

http://www.nestle-aland.com **Nestle-Aland Text**

Vita

Frank Abissi was born in 1957 in Staten Island, NY. He grew up in Connecticut until he was 17 years old when he moved to the Philadelphia, Pennsylvania area. He cultivated his relationship with Jesus Christ as his Saviour beginning at age 17. He attended Upper Bucks Technical School and Bucks County Community College until he decided to attend the Way College of Emporia, Kansas starting in 1980. He graduated in 1983 and went to Des Moines Iowa with his wife, Lena where they ran home Bible fellowships. In 1985 they moved to Grand Rapids, MI. They took a hiatus from running Bible fellowships for several years until they began attending North Kent Bible Church. Frank taught Sunday school and became an Elder in the church. Frank was ordained to the Christian Ministry in January of 2010.

In 2011 Frank began attending Akribos Theological Seminary[126] through distance learning classes and earned a Bachelor of Arts in Theology in 2012.

Frank then began an on-line program through Northwestern Theological Seminary (2013) and earned a Masters of Theology in Biblical Studies in 2014. His Thesis was "A Re-Examination of the Lordship of Jesus Christ: Patronage" which looked at Jesus Christ as a patron which relationship with the believer was not only power and authority but also an intimate relationship, something that was not found in the lordship relationship alone.

In December of 2014 he completed his Doctor of Theology in Biblical Studies, Summa Cum Laude from Northwestern Theological Seminary. His dissertation: "A Philological Examination of the Seven Doctrinal Treatises of the Epistle to the Ephesians" which was published in 2015 by Outskirts Press as ""The Doctrine of Ephesians" a Philological

---

[126] Tipp City, Ohio

Examination". In May of 2016 Frank completed and was conferred the Doctor of Philosophy in Biblical Philology degree from Northwestern Christian University. His dissertation was the topic of this book.

Professionally, Frank has been a professional rock climber, owning Higher Ground Rock Climbing Centre Ltd. in Grand Rapids, MI and Inside Moves Climbing Gym in Byron Center, MI, since 1994. In the past years, Frank's company has taught over 250,000 people various aspects of rock and ice climbing. Frank has climbed all over North America, South America, France, and Switzerland.

Frank and Lena Abissi have two sons, Andrew, a high-school teacher in Grand Rapids and Paul, who works also as a Pro-Rock Climber at Higher Ground. Lena manages a Tax Department and is a Certified Financial Planner®.

When not studying or climbing Frank and Lena enjoy spending time together at their cabin on Owls Head Mountain in the Adirondacks of Upper New York State.

Frank and Lena currently attend Monroe Community Church in Downtown Grand Rapids, MI.

Printed in the United States
By Bookmasters